THE 11:11
CODE

SECRETS
OF THE CONVENT

First published by O-Books, 2008
O-Books is an imprint of John Hunt Publishing Ltd., The Bothy, Deershot Lodge, Park Lane, Ropley,
Hants, SO24 0BE, UK
office1@o-books.net
www.o-books.com

For distributor details and how to order please visit the 'Ordering' section on our website.

Text copyright: Hilary H. Carter 2008

ISBN: 978 1 84694 100 9

A CIP catalogue record for this book is available from the British Library.

Design: Stuart Davies

Printed in the UK by CPI Antony Rowe
Printed in the USA by Offset Paperback Mfrs, Inc

We operate a distinctive and ethical publishing philosophy in all
areas of our business, from our global network of authors to
production and worldwide distribution.

THE 11:11 CODE

SECRETS
OF THE CONVENT

Hilary Carter

BOOKS

Winchester, UK
Washington, USA

CONTENTS

This book is dedicated to John Couzens

(13.11.1943 - 14.09.2004)

Without his help I would never have owned the convent.

He lived for exactly 22,222days…

CHAPTER ONE

Above the door was a handmade wooden board scrawled with the words 'Convento Franciscano. Antiguo.' My Spanish was virtually non-existent but even I could work out it meant this was an old Franciscan convent. Pedro produced a huge key and inserted it into the ornate keyhole, decorated with two eagles looking in opposite directions. On closer inspection I realized it was one eagle with two heads. As he turned the key to unlock the antique, heavy, studded door, peals of bells rang out, a serenade that could be heard for miles. Once a day at midday the church bells on the Catholic church at the top of the road played this tune. It must be exactly noon. I was struck by the synchronicity of the moment.

The key turned easily in the lock and we cautiously entered this wreck of a building. It was in a terrible state. It was a virtual ruin. There was no electricity, gas or water and it had the putrid smell of neglect. It was obvious that nobody had lived there for years. The ceiling in the entrance hall was sagging badly. The convent was built in the traditional style, thick earth walls, with tree trunks laid between two walls to act as a joist and locally grown cane laid across the beams. The hall floor was tiled, although the tiles were ugly. We looked into the first room. It was huge and dark with an earth floor. The ceiling was very high and there was only one window, which was so high up that we could not see out. I wondered if animals had once been kept in there; two mummified cats were lying on the floor. They must have got trapped in the convent. Plaster had fallen off the walls in lots of places, revealing the bare walls, built from a mixture of broken terracotta pottery and stones mixed in with the earth. This room led through to another room of about the same size, with an earth floor. This room too was dark and high. I had a strange sensation as if my skin was crawling. I didn't like this place. We headed upstairs through a beautiful carved door. The carving was the same as the ornate keyhole, with the double-headed eagle. "What a lovely door." I commented.

"It looks like that dates from the fifteenth century. It is certainly very old," Katarina, the German estate agent who had introduced me to this property, assured me.

The staircase was wide and rather grand, marble with delicate wrought iron balustrades. This was in complete contrast to the basic state of the downstairs. Through the classically arched windows halfway up the stairs I could see through to the patio. It was small and dominated by the shadow of the church tower. Part of the convent wall adjoined the church. The upstairs was in slightly better condition, though the floors were ankle deep with a mixture of swallow and pigeon droppings; the swallows had got in through an open window and the peculiar smell of bird droppings permeated the place. I saw a dead rat and several dead birds amongst the droppings. Water had got in through the roof, leaving huge black marks down the walls. The shuttered windows were partially broken. Some of the original interior wooden doors remained, misshapen and showing signs of age, but steeped in character, with no sign of rot in the wood. The doorways were low and the wooden doors very small. There was a large crack in one of the walls and I could see daylight through a hole in the ceiling. The wall here was in a dreadful state, black with mould and damaged beyond repair by decades of rain. The windows were carved from the earth walls, creating a natural window seat at each one. They looked out towards the new apartment building next door, not a very inspiring view. There were six rooms and a bathroom in this part of the convent, though none of them were habitable. They looked to me as if they had last been decorated in the 1930s. The wallpaper was hand printed with blue flowers, and the floors were a particularly unattractive composite marble, the same as in the entrance hall.

We could not get through to the back of the building from here because the upstairs landing floor had totally collapsed and landed in the room below. So we went downstairs and out into the patio. It was overgrown but I could make out an arched window leading through to the church. From here the tower of the adjoining church seemed even more oppressive, casting a dark shadow that had a sinister feel to it. I could see a statue of Jesus on top of the adjoining tower. He had his back to me. Pigeons suddenly flew out of the tower, causing me to start.

Katarina cleared a way through the patio with Pedro's help to get to the back the convent. I spotted a massive spider and decided to go no further. This place had a very odd feel to it. I got the distinct feeling that I was being watched although I couldn't see anyone. All I did know was that this place did not want to be disturbed.

"Come and look Hilary," called Katarina "It's huge." She disappeared out of sight, having fought her way through to access the back part of the building.

"No, I'll wait outside," I called back. The invisible barrier was too powerful to break. No way was I going any further. I couldn't wait to get out of this place, onto the street again. That place was not for me. It would be one huge headache and I did not have the patience, desire or resources to tackle a project like that. It would take years and a massive amount of money to get the place habitable. It wasn't beautiful either. There was no doubt that it was filled with character and saturated with history but it had been unoccupied for far too long.

I pushed the heavy door aside and stepped out into the street with a sigh of relief. There was definitely something oppressive about that place.

"It's awful, isn't it," I said to my boyfriend Anthony.

"It's a major renovation project, but it's a holy place. Lots of praying has gone on in there. Good place to teach yoga."

"It's a dump. It's in an awful state. They shouldn't have let it go like that."

I was disappointed and I felt despondent. Back to square one. It wasn't going to be as easy as I had thought finding a place to run yoga courses. But it was my dream and I did not want to let go of the dream.

Katarina could see I was not impressed. She was standing in the dark entrance hall discussing the price with Pedro. He was working in pesetas and she was trying to convert it into euros. She said she was not sure what the price was but said she would let me know in due course.

"Do you have anything else to show me?" I asked hopefully.

"No there is nothing else at the moment but I have your email address so I will keep you informed if I hear of anything."

We parted company outside the door and Anthony and I wandered down the street towards the town square. The roads here were extremely narrow. The road of the convent, Calle de Los Meridas, was not much wider than the width of one car. It was a quiet town. Nobody was in a hurry and nor were we. We wandered despondently down to the bottom of the narrow, gently sloping road. It opened out into a large square and we headed towards the café in the corner. We sat outside under the canopy drinking 'mosto', the locally produced grape juice, and soaked up the peace and quiet. A circular fountain was flowing and two small children stood playing with the water.

"Do you think it's worth considering?" asked Anthony.

"No way. It needs so much work. Anyway, I didn't like it," I insisted. "I know it was a convent but there's something about that place that I didn't like. I can't put my finger on it. It's just a feeling."

The next day we left this small town in the mountains of Andalucia, southern Spain, and drove back down to the coast to relax by the sea. We returned to England a couple of days later. Shortly after we arrived back in England an email arrived from Katarina to let me know that the asking price of the convent was around £85,000. It was difficult to get an exact figure as the prices in this part of Spain were still quoted in pesetas. The pesetas have to be converted to euros and from euros into pounds. It was a reasonable price considering the uniqueness of the convent.

Returning to England and going back to my normal day to day routine, I began to think that finding a place in Spain might be impossible at this time in my life. I could not keep popping out to Spain. For a start, I couldn't afford it, and, as a self-employed yoga teacher, it meant I had to keep canceling my classes. Canceled classes meant no income. Maybe I had set myself an impossible dream?

A few days later I started to think about the convent again. I hadn't even seen half of it. I didn't know exactly how big it was. I wondered how much of the layout I could remember? I picked up a pen and paper and started sketching a floor plan. I started by drawing the entrance hall with the two rooms on the right. Then I tried to work out where the courtyard fitted in. As soon as I put pen to paper I noticed the bells ringing at the church down the road. There was a Catholic church about two hundred yards from my house. That was strange. The bells could not have been striking the hour because it had just passed the hour. I noted on my digital watch that it was exactly 11:11am. I thought that there must have been a wedding, or maybe a funeral? Then I remembered how the bells had tolled midday when Pedro had put the key in the lock at the old convent. Moments after noticing the tolling of the church bells, my telephone rang. It was the estate agent in England. I was selling a small one roomed studio flat I had bought after my divorce a few years ago. It had been on the market for quite a while but I had not had an offer. I answered the phone. "We have some good news for you," said the agent. "We have just had an offer on your studio. They have made an offer of the full asking price."

I accepted immediately of course. That was the first offer I had had and it was for the full asking price – £90,000 pounds, enough to buy the convent and pay the solicitors' fees. That would have been perfect if I had wanted to go ahead and make an offer on the convent. I had not even thought about the convent for days and as soon as I focused my mind on it, things had started to happen. I take notice of coincidences. To my way of thinking, coincidences are signs. I thought about the signs around this convent. There were the tolling bells at noon as the key was put in the lock. The bells on my local church were ringing at 11:11am, the timing of that phone call with the offer. And then there was the amount of the offer on my flat. Not just one coincidence, but a few.

I decided I could not ignore the signs so I emailed Katarina to ask her if she knew of any builders in Spain who might be able to give me an idea of the cost of renovations on the convent. She replied at 11:11am the following day. I was stunned when I saw what time her reply had come through. That was too much to ignore. The bells had rung at 11:11 then the email had come through at 11:11. Something was going on but I didn't know what. I knew I would have to take action because of these coincidences, so I rang Katarina to ask whether the vendors would drop the price to 100,000 euros. I was not committing myself to anything at this stage, simply collecting information. I could raise a maximum of £100,000 and I would need some money left over to renovate the property. A few days later I was sitting at the computer writing when Katarina rang with the reply.

"Hilary, I have spoken with the owners and we have a new price."

"Did they agree to drop to 100,000 euros?"

"No. They are giving the price in pesetas. This part of Spain you know is very slow, very backward. They do not like to work in euros. So the price they give me is in pesetas. I convert this price to pounds it is £77,500."

"Okay thanks Katarina, I'll think about it and get back to you."

That would leave me about £20,000 to renovate the place. No way would that be enough. It was in such a state that I reckoned £50,000 was a more realistic figure. That was a relief, because I didn't like the old convent. I was only pursuing it because of the coincidences.

Deepak Chopra calls coincidences 'signs' and in his book *Synchrodestiny* he suggests that signs are the language of our higher consciousness. However, I knew I could not afford to follow this particular sign and I was pleased about that. Maybe if they'd dropped to 100,000 euros I could have just about managed to afford to buy it and perhaps renovate part of it. I wondered how far off my offer of 100,000 euros £77,500 was? I typed 77,500GBP into the currency converter on the internet. I wish I hadn't.

Because the conversion came up as 111,100 euros.

CHAPTER TWO

I am often asked how I found the convent. My reply is that I did not find the convent. The convent found me. Looking back, I don't think I had any choice in the matter. Like a fly caught in a spiders' web, it wasn't until I had actually bought the convent and found myself caught in its dark web that I really began to realize what I had let myself in for. By then it was too late and there could be no turning back. I was going to be taken to the edge of sanity, for only by walking in that dangerous place could I find the answers to my questions and only by thinking at the edge of my mind could I think the unthinkable – that the world as I knew it and the information and knowledge I had been fed was, on the whole, utter rubbish. I had been conditioned and the time had come for my conditioning to be undone.

So that is how it came about. That is how the convent found me. That is how the convent spoke to me. Through numbers (especially 11:11) and coincidences.

Now there are undoubtedly going to be those people who think I am crazy because I decided to spend my entire wealth, accumulated over many years of hard work, on a wreck of a convent because the agent sent me an email at 11:11am. And I have to admit that I can see their point of view. Just a few short years ago I would have thought the same.

11:11 first made an appearance in my life in the mid 1990s. A group of people I knew were organizing a trip to the ancient stone circle at Stonehenge for a world peace ceremony. This was to take place on 11th November at 11am. This is Armistice Day, the anniversary of the official end of World War I, November 11, 1918. It commemorates the armistice signed between the Allies and Germany at Compiègne, France, for the cessation of hostilities on the Western Front, which took effect at eleven o'clock in the morning — the eleventh hour of the eleventh day of the eleventh month of the year.

If I'm honest, I only really went along for a day out. I don't remember a lot about the trip, other than we weren't allowed into Stonehenge and ended up trying to meditate on the grass verge outside, squeezed between the high metal fencing and a busy road. Stonehenge is in the middle of the countryside in Wiltshire, England. The 11:11 ceremony involved passing round a sword that supposedly had a link with King Arthur, and I knew that we were linking up in thought with other groups of peace workers around the world. I knew that the ceremony was something to do with 11:11 because of the day it was taking place.

Several years later 11:11 made another appearance. That time it was a major appearance. My boyfriend, Anthony, an acupuncturist, decided to go out for a day in the country. Again it was November 11th. Anthony owned an ancient old Mercedes car that was heading for the scrap heap and this was to be our last journey in this car. It had well over 100,000 miles on the clock.

"Where should we take it for its last trip?" he asked me.

"I think we should head out of town on the dual carriageway and deep into the Dorset countryside. How about Knowlton?" I suggested. Knowlton is a Bronze Age earth circle in the middle of which lies the ruin of a fourteenth century church.

The weather was not brilliant, sunshine and clouds; it could go either way. Typical English weather. We could have a beautiful crisp, sunny day or it could rain. By the time we got to the end of the dual carriageway at Ringwood it looked like the clouds were going to win out and it might rain.

"I don't think we should go that far, Anthony. Look at the weather. Let's just go to that little church at Ellingham and have a sit inside there in the silence."

Anthony agreed with me. It's only a couple of miles further on and Ellingham church has an atmosphere about it that only long history can give. We turned off the main road into the dead end road leading to the church. The oak trees that lined the narrow country lane still had some of their leaves, yellow and brown, waiting for a storm to dislodge them. We pulled in on a small gravel drive near the gate of the churchyard.

"There you are car. This is the last place you are going to visit."

Anthony turned off the engine and we sat in silence.

"Look," said Anthony. "Look how many miles it has done."

I leaned over and looked at the milometer and gasped. Exactly 111100.

I looked at Anthony. Our eyes met in wonder. But there was more.

"Look at the trip meter." The trip meter is the small meter that records how many miles you drive on a tank of petrol, or you can set it to record how many miles on a particular journey. Anthony always used to set it when he put petrol in because it was a very thirsty car and we didn't go out in it very often. He liked to keep an eye on the petrol consumption.

I looked at the trip meter. One hundred and eleven miles; 111. I didn't know whether to laugh or cry. Quite frankly I felt spooked.

"And the clock," Anthony stated. 11:11am.

I didn't cry but my heart started beating really hard as if to remind me that no, I was not dreaming, this was actually happening. I can handle coincidence when it crops up in a reasonable way but this was beyond reason. When I got out of the car a huge gust of wind lifted the scattered leaves from the path and they swirled around me like a mini tornado, then the wind disappeared and they fell to the ground again. We walked towards the church; my legs were a bit shaky as I walked unsteadily through the graveyard towards the church door. I lifted the latch on the arched, oak door and entered the ancient stone church. A closed bible was laid on the pulpit and I opened it at random. It opened at Matthew chapter 11. My eyes scanned the page for verse 11. Matthew 11.11.

'I tell you this; never has there appeared on earth a mother's son greater than John the Baptist, and yet the least in the kingdom of Heaven is greater than he.'

What did that mean? Was that a message? I had never found the bible an easy book to understand. I found obscurity difficult. I liked my t's crossed and my i's dotted. I made a mental note to do some research on John the Baptist on the internet. Following what had happened with all those 11's in the car I was taking 11 seriously.

I have to point out that it was Anthony who noticed these coincidences. He was the one who was so aware. He noticed these things because he lives in the moment and not in his head like a lot of people. Had I been in the car alone I might well have completely overlooked the 11:11 on the clock, trip meter and milometer. Anthony lives in full awareness, which enables him to take note of everything that is happening in each moment.

"What does it mean, this 11:11?" I asked him.

"It's a sign."

"A sign of what?"

"It's a sign that we are on the right path. We are in the right place at the right time."

"But who's giving us a sign and how do they get it there. How do they put it into the car like that?"

Anthony smiled enigmatically. He is a man of few words at the best of times and he didn't answer me.

"Anthony. Help me out here. I don't like it. It's too weird".

"It's magic."

"Yes I know it's magic. But who is the magician? And why is it 11? Why that number?"

"I've told you before. The right rhythm, the right number, the right proportion. That's how we get out of here."

By 'here' he meant life. Like me, he believes in reincarnation and like me, he doesn't want to keep coming back to earth.

"You'll see. Just allow things to unfold in their own time and you will understand what is going on."

"You don't understand either," I retorted. He retreated into silence. Maybe it had frightened him too. Or maybe I'm not ready to hear the truth? As usual, he was right and it would just be a case of allowing things to unfold in their own time. All I could see at that moment was the fact that something beyond me or Anthony was happening. It was happening in a way that had come right into our everyday lives. This was not some theory or belief system. This was something going on right in front of our eyes for us to see. This was not some vague ethereal experience where we could think our imagination was taking over, such as seeing a ghost. No. Something beyond our conscious control was manifesting in a way that could not be ignored or denied.

From that day on I was definitely tuned in to 11:11. Whenever it appeared I stopped and took notice. I knew that it was something special and that it meant something, but I didn't know what. So when the email from Katarina came through I realized that the convent was a part of the 11:11. I did have a choice, though. I could have simply ignored the sign and not pursued the purchase of the convent. But when I took all the other coincidences into consideration, I thought something big was happening. Did I have the courage to follow the signs? Was I brave enough to ignore my rational, sensible mind? I did not allow myself time to think about it or I would probably have reasoned myself out of it. I took a huge leap of faith and phoned Katarina.

"I've decided to buy the convent."

Katarina was a bit surprised at the speed and suddenness of my decision. After all, I had only ever seen the front few rooms of the place. I was buying a place that I hadn't even fully seen.

"So, I think you have a good deal. You will need to pay the price in euros. The price will not drop from this price." She didn't really have to tell me that. She didn't know it, but this was the only price it could be!

Naturally the offer was accepted and I duly sent a deposit of 11,120 euros. I had used a currency converter on the internet which had shown the 111,100 euros. A slight fluctuation in the exchange rate between British pounds and the euro had increased the price to 111,200 euros, but I have learned that the 11:11 can appear as 11 or 111 and is equally valid as a sign.

It was done. The deposit was paid so now I was committed to purchasing the convent. The Spanish system of buying and selling houses is different to the English system. Once the deposit is paid, the purchaser is committed to the sale. I had three months to get out to Spain to complete the purchase. If I pulled out now I would lose my deposit. What had I done? I decided just to let the wheels turn now that they had been set in motion. There was no going back. I needed to have faith that I had done the right thing. My studio flat was being bought by first time buyers who had their mortgage arranged, so I assumed that would go through smoothly. Famous last words.

Early in July I got a phone call from my solicitor who informed me that the buyers' solicitor had found a problem with the lease on the studio. It would take several weeks to sort out. That was awful news. I was due to go out to Spain ten days later to pay the balance and collect the deeds. I had left it right to the limit of my three month deadline. What was I going to do? There was no way that the studio sale would have gone through before my Spanish deadline. I had no other money and would not have been able to raise a loan. If I couldn't raise £50,000 I would lose my deposit. I racked my brains to think of anybody I know who might have fifty thousand sitting in a bank account somewhere. Obviously the list of possible candidates was quite short. In fact my list consisted of one person. My cousin John. Since my father had died some years ago my cousin had been my rock. I always turned to him to discuss the type of things that I would have discussed with my father. I asked him the questions I would have asked my father.

"John, I have a favour to ask you. A really big favour."

Even as I was asking I realized that this was a huge favour.

" I wonder if you could lend me fifty thousand pounds. I will need it in three days time at the most. I have to allow time for it to clear my English account and then to be transferred to my Spanish account which the estate agent in Spain has set up for me."

"Fifty thousand?" asked John.

"Yes, I know it's a bit of a tall order but basically if you can't lend it to me then my Spanish project cannot go ahead."

John was as cool as can be. It was as if I had asked him for a fiver.

"It just so happens that I have just transferred a large amount into my regular bank account because I am about to start work on my project."

John was renovating a sixteenth century house in the South Downs in Sussex, England.

"So that should be no problem. I can come down with my cheque book in a couple of days."

And so it was that the project was saved.

"I'll pay you back as soon as I possibly can," I assured him.

"Oh don't you worry about that," he replied.

"Have you told your girlfriend you are giving me this money?" I asked.

"It's my money and I will do what I want with it. We will keep it a secret just between the two of us," he said.

John had always had a strong independent streak and I noticed a defiance in his voice. He had made it to the age of 60 without ever walking down the aisle. Handsome, intelligent, interesting, generous, wealthy and the most thoroughly wonderful man you could wish to meet, he had been pursued unsuccessfully by many women.

"Listen, if I die you can have the money out of my estate, not that my estate will be worth that much."

I picked up a photo of the convent from the pile of photos I had been showing him and scribbled some writing on the back: 'IN THE EVENT OF MY SUDDEN DEATH PLEASE PAY JOHN BACK THE MONEY HE GAVE ME.'

John laughed. "You are funny! What are the chances of you suddenly dropping down dead!" Little did I realize that within a few short weeks it was he who would be dead.

CHAPTER THREE

The convent, like all Spanish properties, came with an 'escitura' which is like the deeds to the house. It was all in Spanish of course, so Katarina had to translate it for me.

"... and the property has conferred on it ancient lights which means that it has a right to the light and nobody can build within two meters of the walls..."

I sat up and took notice. My home in Bournemouth, Dorset also had ancient lights bestowed upon it. This was interesting.

Katarina continued her translation: "... the property being a former Franciscan monastery and comprising one third of the whole, one part being a museum and the other part a private house. With the property comes a fountain and the right to constantly flowing table water..."

"A fountain? It has a fountain? I didn't see any fountain." I was so excited. I love fountains!

"That's what it says here so there must be one. Maybe it has been closed up."

We were sitting in the waiting room of the lawyers office in Ugijar, the small town in the Alpujarra mountains of southern Spain where I had discovered the convent. The air was thick with cigarette smoke. Three other groups of people were waiting to see the lawyer. He didn't appear to have an appointment system. It seemed to be a case of first come, first served, and we were next in line.

"What museum. It says one third is a museum?"

Katarina looked at me impatiently. She was rushing through the escitura because we were next and she wanted to be sure that I knew what I was buying before I signed any papers.

"I will tell you later."

She proceeded to translate from Spanish to English and had literally just finished the last sentence when we were ushered into the lawyer's office. The documents were signed and the money was handed over. There was no messing around. The whole process took less that ten minutes. Then came the moment I had been waiting for. I was handed the great big ancient key. I wrapped my fingers round the heavy metal key and felt a strange sense of familiarity. It felt comfortable in my hand and I had a strong sense of the key belonging to me. Now I was the owner of the convent and I suddenly felt very excited. As we stood outside the lawyer's office in the burning sun I asked Katarina about the museum.

"You see the big tower beside your convent?"

"Yes I know the tower, the one with the statue of Jesus on top."

"Yes. Well this is a museum. It used to be a part of the convent. It belongs to a lawyer who does not live in Ugijar. He has spent a lot of money making renovations and now he has created this museum for the people of the town."

I added 'visit the museum' to the list of things to do that I was carrying round in my head.

There were handshakes all round and I headed off alone to open the door of my new acquisition. I was alone because a few weeks earlier I had split up with Anthony after a five year relationship; something between us had just died. He would not be joining me in Spain.

I slowly walked the few hundred meters to the convent in the summer heat. It was August and the temperatures were well into the nineties. Nobody moved fast. I passed the bar where men sat drinking in the shade. Their eyes followed me. I stuck out like a sore thumb in this small town with my fair hair, green eyes and colorful flowing skirt. For once in my life I felt tall because most of the local population were short and dark haired. Walking the length of the high street took less than two minutes, even at a leisurely pace. Past the bank, the small supermarket, the 'department store', the butcher, another supermarket, another bar, another bank and an olive oil shop.

I took a sharp left, down the one-way street that led to the town square and stopped outside the convent. MY convent. For the first time, I put the key in the lock and turned the key. The church bells rang. The timing was impeccable. That was the second time it had happened. Now I really knew there was something weird going on. The door swung open slowly and I stepped inside and closed it behind me. I was alone in the convent. A sudden flutter of wings startled me. A swallow flew out of the door and onto the patio. I followed it with my eyes and looked upwards as it flew away. I could see where an arched door had been blocked in on the side of the church. My patio was two-thirds of the original patio, the other third belonged to the neighbor. Somewhere on this patio was supposed to be the fountain, but I couldn't see it. It was so overgrown. This was only the second time I had been here. Now I could have a look at what I had bought. I tried not to let my heart sink. I stood and looked around. Once again I got the feeling I was being watched, yet I knew there was nobody there. Another flutter of wings alarmed me as several pigeons took flight. They disappeared into the tower of the church, obviously where they were roosting. The tower of the adjoining church was built from thin red bricks and a flint like stone not unlike the flint of my cousin John's house in Sussex. Most of the walls in my section had been rendered but I could see in parts where the render had fallen off revealing the much older building materials underneath. My convent had been built in the same way as the tower so I assumed it must have been connected to the tower in some way. Alterations had been made over the years and I could make out the faint outline of arched windows. I wondered why they had filled in the windows? The roof was old red pan tiles, except that they were not very red any more, coated as they were with lichen. I could see a door beyond the patio but to get to it would have meant clambering through the undergrowth and I was not dressed for that. I was wearing a silk skirt in an effort to stay cool. I could do that another day. Something tickled my sandaled foot and I realized I was standing in the path of some giant ants. Lifting my foot sharply I flicked an ant off and I followed it with my eyes as it landed in the eye socket of a skeleton of a large cat. Yuck! I hastily retreated into the entrance hall and made my way upstairs. This was the least dilapidated part of the convent. Even so, it was completely uninhabitable. Stopping on the way upstairs, I examined the carved door more closely. It had been beautifully carved with a two-headed eagle. Somebody had varnished the door in a ghastly orange varnish. That would have to come off. Wandering towards the window on the first floor landing, I looked out onto the new building next door. It was three floors high and dominated the modest proportions of the two-storey convent. I tried to imagine what the outlook would have been like before this was built. It would probably have been open land. A garden or an orchard maybe? A woman was shouting in Spanish. A child cried in response. I could hear dogs barking and chickens clucking. There was a perfect unbroken egg lying on the highest pile of pigeon droppings in what used to be the living room. I picked it up, wondering how old it was. For some reason I thought of Anthony.

"What does an egg represent?" said Anthony's voice in my mind.

'Potential' came the immediate answer.

I held firmly onto the graceful wrought iron banister, as I carefully picked my way over the bird and animal droppings back to the ground floor. I ought to have been brave and fought my way through the undergrowth to see the rest of the building, I still didn't know what lay at the back of the convent. But once again I felt a powerful resistance and I just wanted to be out of the place.

"It's a holy place," I remembered Anthony's words. I was having a bit of a struggle. I wanted it to be a holy place and I wanted it to be special and I was trying to imagine that this was what I felt. But it was no good. I could not deny this uncomfortable feeling I got when I was in there. I unlocked the door from the inside and stepped out once more into the bright sunlit street. My eyes tried to adjust to the dramatic change; the convent was dark and the entrance hall was windowless. Walking up the side of the property and examining the outside walls I could see that the walls were built on stone foundations. The place was huge. The wall went back at least 40 meters, ending at a padlocked metal gate which led onto a private garden. Again I could make out arches where windows had been blocked in. A fig tree lived precariously on the wall, its roots grasping onto the earth at the top of the wall where it met the roof. There were only two floors to the building and it was exactly as I had remembered it from my first visit, a wreck. But this wreck had drawn me to it. It had found me through coincidence and the number 11:11.

I knew that I must stay focused and grounded. I was going to need a builder to renovate the front part of the convent so that at least I would have somewhere to live. Katarina the estate agent had introduced me to an English man who had recently bought a property in a nearby village. It was through him that I was introduced to Emilio.

"Please could you take a look at the convent and give me an idea of the cost of making three of the rooms habitable, and putting in a bathroom and a kitchen," I asked him. "I'll leave you the key and when I come back in October we can have a chat." I handed over the precious key. There was only one key in existence. It was not as if I could get another one of these cut in the corner shop. To duplicate this key would require a blacksmith making a pressed mould.

I returned to England for a few weeks to make my final arrangements for my move to Spain. I had only been back in England for a few days when I received a phone call from my mother. "Hilary, I have got some bad news." Her voice was weak and tearful. I couldn't imagine what might have happened.

"You're not going to believe it. I can't believe it. Your cousin John has died suddenly from a heart attack."

I was in the living room at home. I sat down sharply on the sofa as my knees gave way.

"But he can't have died. He wasn't ill."

He was never ill. He was fit, strong and active and only 60 years old.

"It was very sudden and unexpected," my mother continued.

"What happened?"

"He was out on his digger digging ditches down the side of the track when he felt unwell. He went home for lunch, lay down and was dead within the hour. He'd had a massive heart attack; there was no way he could have survived."

All sorts of thoughts went swimming through my head. To die so suddenly and so young. My dear cousin. To me he was brother, father and friend rolled into one. He had always been in my life and he had always been the one I turned to when I needed help. He had never let me down. Not once. I would miss him terribly. And what about the money he had lent me? This was our secret and now our secret would come out.

My mother had more to say. "He was married last week."

In the time between giving me the money and dropping down dead, John had married his girlfriend in a secret ceremony. John the confirmed bachelor died less than two weeks after walking up the aisle. He was to be buried in his wedding suit.

My mind was reeling as I tried to take in this sudden turn of events. Questions kept popping into my mind. How come he had died so soon after getting married? Why had he married in secret? If he had died a few weeks ago, I wouldn't be the owner of the convent.

I tried to take conscious control of my mind. Sudden death is a difficult thing to deal with. If someone is ill and they know they are going to die, then there is time to say what has to be said, to deal with what has to be dealt with, and to say goodbye. But when the death is sudden and unexpected, it is a shock.

"He was married on the Friday morning, on the third of September," my mother continued. "It must be one of the shortest marriages ever in our family."

This was the 14th. The relevance of those dates hit me immediately. It was indeed a very short marriage. John had been married for exactly 11 days.

CHAPTER FOUR

Back once more in England I pondered my situation. I was now the owner of the convent. It was quite obvious to me that I would not be able to oversee the renovations of the convent whilst living in England. I would need to be living in Ugijar to be able to keep a close eye on things. I would have to move to Spain. A plan began to form in my mind. I could let out my home in England and live off the rent, supplemented by running some yoga classes in Spain. All I would need to do would be to find somewhere to live in Ugijar. By the end of one year the convent would be habitable, with a studio for teaching yoga, so I would be able to run residential courses for a week at a time. Perfect!

When I mentioned this plan to my friends they are pretty unanimous in their reactions.

"That's a brave thing to do, to go out to Spain and undertake a huge project like that on your own."

Brave? I didn't think so. I thought it was exciting.

The English man Katarina had put me in touch with had also bought a property in the province of Granada, 3000 meters above Ugijar in a village called Valor. Within the villa was a brand new two-bedroom apartment and he had offered to rent it to me.

I booked my flight to Almeria for Oct 7th at 11am. The luggage allowance was only 20 kilos so I would just have to live with the bare necessities for a year. Unfortunately the flight was delayed for six hours so I arrived in Spain having missed the last bus by several hours. I had no choice but to rent a car and drive up the mountain roads in the dark, on the righthand side of the road, on roads that I don't know. The journey took more than three hours because I got lost. I was so thankful to lay my head down in my rented apartment that night.

I woke up late the next morning and opened the window shutters.

The bright mountain sun was filtering through the olive tree outside and cast a dappled light onto my bed. Stepping outside, a salamander scurried past my bare feet. The vivid pink of the bougainvillea just outside the back door shocked me with the vividness of its pink hue. From the terrace I could see the rolling hills of the Alpujarra mountains. Down below lay the whitewashed town of Ugijar nestled in the valley, surrounded by the dramatic red cliffs, rather like a mini grand canyon. It was so picturesque. Ugijar, at 600 meters above sea level was high, but Valor, although only five kilometers from Ugijar was 300 meters higher. I breathed in the clear mountain air and marveled at the fact that yesterday I was in the dirt and noise of central London and today I was high up a mountain.

The week I arrived was the week of the local fiesta. Ugijar has the biggest fiesta in the area. The Alpujarras is a mountain range that makes up the foothills of the Sierra Nevada mountains, the highest mountain range in Spain. These unspoilt hills are dotted with small white washed villages. This area is way behind the rest of Spain because it has been isolated for so long. Franco hated this part of Spain and deliberately kept the people poor. No money was sent to this area and so the people eked out a living from the land.

The first thing that I discovered was that Ugijar is small, with a population of about 2000 to 2500 people. There was one main road that ran through the middle of town, lined with mature plane trees. It was quite a narrow road, just wide enough for two cars to pass each other plus there were parking spaces for about fifteen or twenty cars. The parade of shops on one side of the road were quite modern and there was a shiny pink and white tiled pavement. The other side of the road had older properties such as the old pharmacy, the hermitage, the church and a very grand old house opposite the church. There was one hotel called the Vidana. Downstairs was the bar with a large terrace and upstairs were a few rooms with balconies overlooking the main road. A man was standing on the wrought iron balcony smoking a cigarette and I saw him see me. A large banner was tied to the railing of his balcony. On it was written 'Golden Cock Award 1988'. Apparently this is a food award, rather like the Egon Ronay awards.

In the back streets were the old places, Arabic in origin, dating back to 800AD. The Moorish influence could still be seen in the shape of the doorways, and glimpses into inner courtyards. None of the ones I saw had a fountain like the convent. At least I hoped it had a fountain. I still hadn't found it amongst the undergrowth. The convent was in the Moorish part of the town, where the streets were so narrow that some houses had a narrow bridge between two houses at first floor level, where some of the rooms of a house were on the other side of the road! The sound of running water revealed the location of a small fuente, or fountain. Often these were in small plazas where one could sit and watch the world go by, the sound of the gently flowing water adding to the relaxed feel of the place.

The town was an eclectic mixture of ancient and modern. It had been inhabited by the Romans, Phoenicians and Visigoths before the Moorish conquest of southern Spain in the eighth century. This region was the last refuge of the Moors and their influence was everywhere. At least that is what I was told. So I had the idea that the area was populated by the Moors and only the Moors. Later I would find out that in fact this town had been a rich cultural mix of faiths and nationalities.

There were very old properties and quite a lot of new buildings. In one part of town there was a sizable gypsy community. The people were a lot darker. The gypsy community does most of the menial work such as sweeping the streets. Others worked out of town in the fields, planting and picking crops of herbs for herb teas. Some were builders' labourers, skilled at their work, plastering and building in the traditional way. A lot of them didn't work. There were the old gypsy houses and the new ones, all segregated from the rest of the population. The old area was shocking. I came across it one day by accident. I was looking for a sacred well that I had read about but I couldn't ask the locals where it was because of my lack of Spanish. So I decided to look for it myself, reasoning that the town was so small that I was bound to come across it sooner or later. I wandered up a narrow side road on the other side of town, away from the convent. The roads were not very good in this part of town but they suddenly got much worse and the potholes got bigger. The houses up that road were tiny and some of them appeared uninhabited. The word hovel sprung to mind. A few of the houses had crumbled to the ground and there were large areas of wasteland. Here and there small groups of people stood in silence, watching me walk by. An old woman sat on her doorstep and glared, as if I was trespassing. There was a menacing air about the place. Suddenly a pack of wild dogs appeared from nowhere and ran straight towards me, barking furiously. As the dogs started to bark people appeared in doorways to see what was going on. I backtracked as fast as I could but the dogs had surrounded me and I dared not walk too fast in case I got attacked. 'Don't make eye contact'. I remembered this piece of advice I had heard from somewhere so I desperately tried not to look in their direction. I prayed that I don't get bitten because the chances were high that some of these neglected creatures were rabid. That was my introduction to the gypsy area of town. Scary! But I found the well in a side road behind a metal gate. On the floor of this tiny room, not more than three meters square, was a well decorated with flowers. 'Pozo de La Virgen' said the small plaque on the wall, 'Well of the Virgin'.

Just opposite the well was another room, slightly larger. I looked through the metal grill of the wooden door and there was a highly decorated statue, surrounded by fresh flowers. This must be the local saint.

The fiesta is an annual event. I soon discovered the real meaning of fiesta. This is the week when everyone lets their hair down. The whole concept of 'time' goes out of the window. People stay up all night or sleep all day, adults and children alike. Almost anything goes. The entire town is decked out in flags. But the highlight of the fiesta is the procession of the saint. The patron saint of Ugijar is Saint Martirio. She is also the patron saint of the whole of the Alpujarras, which is what makes this fiesta such an important one. This small room near the holy well I had discovered is where the effigy of the saint is kept. At fiesta time she is moved to the church, and the highlight of the fiesta is when she is taken from the church, down to the town square and back again. She weighs an absolute ton and it takes at least 20 people to carry her. This is no mean feat in the baking hot sun. I was delighted to discover that the procession would be going right past the convent so I decided to watch from my first floor balcony. First I needed to find the key.

I had left the key with Emilio so that he could give me an estimate for the renovations. Now all I had to do was find him so that I could get into the convent. Ugijar is a very traditional Spanish town and only three businesses are owned by foreigners. The internet café is owned by a Spanish speaking South American woman and her Swedish husband, a German man owns an artistic, slightly alternative shop, and the last bar on the main road is run by an English couple. They were bound to know Emilio because Emilio's girlfriend was English. I ordered a coffee at the bar from a tall blonde woman.

"I'm looking for Emilio the builder. Do you know him? He has the key to the convent."

"Oh you must be Hilary. You own the convent."

"Yes I do. I asked Emilio to take a look at it and give me an idea of the cost of renovations."

"Yes he told us all about it. My husband is going to be working on the project. He used to be Clerk of Works for Lambeth Council in London."

This piece of information came as quite a shock to me. I hadn't even given Emilio the job, let alone given him permission to employ anyone else.

"I've got the key here. It's kept behind the bar."

She handed me the key and I took it possessively.

"I'll look after it now thanks."

I drank my coffee and left. I'd been in town for a few days and this would be the first time I had been in the convent since I was last here in August. I got a shock when I opened the door. There were loads of scaffolding poles, a cement mixer and tools of various types stacked in the entrance hall. Emilio was obviously ready to start work. All I had asked for was a quote!

I made my way upstairs and onto the first floor balcony where I would have the perfect view. I waited. Then the bells in the church started to ring. They were not ringing in a melodious way, but in a fast, repetitive way, loudly and urgently. The hair on the back of my neck instantly stood up on end and my heart began to thud. There was something in that particular rhythm of the bells that touched a raw nerve. I heard a band approaching and looked up the road to my left. The band was playing a slow, lilting melody. A small boy dressed in robes walked in front of the priest. He was swinging a huge incense burner and the incense wafted down the road and filled the street. Then the statue of Nuestra Señora del Martirio, patron saint of the Alpujarras appeared. She was being carried by a group of people, mostly men, their faces wet with perspiration. Slowly they swung the saint from side to side. She was mounted on a platform, richly decorated with flowers and ribbons. Behind her a vast crowd of people walked, all carrying candles. They processed down either side of the street and when they reached the convent the entire procession came to a halt. Standing at first floor level on my balcony I was at exactly the same level as Martirio. There I was, standing eye to eye with an effigy of a saint, intoxicated by the incense wafting up from the huge incense burner. I felt as though I was being given a personal message. There was a pause. The band had stopped playing, and in that pause, in that sacred space, as I stood alone in the convent, it is as if time was suspended. In that pause, that pivotal moment, I realized beyond any doubt that there was something very strange going on here. I didn't yet know what, but it was something supernatural.

Suddenly the moment passed, the band started up again and the saint moved on. The men, women and children carrying the candles walked on, leaving a trail of candle wax on the street. They did not have far to go. Just to the bottom of my road, Calle de los Meridas. Maybe this name has the same source as the word meridian, meaning 'the great circle on the celestial sphere passing through the north and south poles'.

At the bottom of the road is the town square where Anthony and I had sat drinking grape juice on the day that we had first entered the convent. For a fleeting moment I wondered whether the convent had anything to do with us splitting up for until we had stepped inside the convent together, it had been our intention to marry. 'Live in the moment'. There were Anthony's words in my head again and they brought me back to the here and now. The procession paused in the square then followed the lower road back to the church. The annual outing of the saint would soon be over. Down in the square a fire had been lit and a huge paella was being cooked for everybody. It was free, as was the beer up in the church square, paid for by the town hall out of the rates.

There was a market for the five days of the fiesta, with stalls selling leather bags, paintings, handicrafts, wood carvings, metal work and clothes. Quite a few of the stallholders were Africans who had come over from North Africa, just across the water. North Africa could be seen on a clear day from the next village up from Valor, Nechite. A direct ferry went from nearby Almeria to the north African coast. The stallholders selling baked potato were gypsies. I didn't know if they were local gypsies or not. There was also a fairground in town, with dodgems and big rides. Most of the young people were hanging out at the fair. Here the rules of the dodgems were in complete contrast to the rules of the dodgems in England. In England behavior on the dodgems is strictly controlled. No standing, no deliberate bumping. Here the idea was to drive as fast as possible and to hit as many cars as possible, as hard as possible. Three to a car was not unusual. The third person simply stood on the back, hanging on with one hand. By the end of the week most of the youngsters had legs that were black and blue with bruises. I heard that someone had lost a foot a few years ago.

Every morning the dawn was greeted by the loudest bangers I had ever heard. The dogs in town went crazy, barking and whining in terror. The earth shook and the noise bounced off the hills and reverberated through the entire valley. This reminded everyone that it was fiesta time and it was time to wake up and continue partying, though judging from the noise throughout the night, lots of people had not stopped partying the night before. During the fiesta the schools were shut and children stayed out well into the early hours.

CHAPTER FIVE

For several days following the fiesta Ugijar was like a ghost town, discarded boxes and bottles and debris left lying in the street, blowing around in the gentle breeze. Even the street cleaners had gone to bed to recover, catching up on sleep and nursing hangovers. The stall-holders and the fair had packed up and moved on to the next fiesta. Nobody was about and nothing was open. It was quite eerie.

Monday came and suddenly life was back to normal. Although I was living in Valor, I spent quite a lot of my time in Ugijar which had much better facilities than Valor. In Ugijar there was a 24 hour medical center, two dentists, a few lawyers, four small supermarkets, two bakers, two hotels, two restaurants, 18 bars, one small department store with an upstairs and one elevator in a three storied block of recently built flats. This was the first elevator in town and the builder was very proud of this fact!

There was also the daily indoor market that sold fruit, vegetables, fish, and eggs. Most of the produce was local though a certain amount had come from the nearby towns of Berja or El Ejido. Coming down to land at Almeria airport, the nearest airport to Ugijar, it was as if one was landing in the midst of a sea of plastic. As far as the eye could see, plastic sheeting glinted in the sunlight. This is the greenhouse of Europe. Here, in huge plastic greenhouses, fruit and vegetables are grown intensively. This is what has made Almeria the wealthiest province in Spain. Massive amounts of money can be made for it is possible to grow three crops in one year. There were a few 'plasticos', as they are known locally, in the area of Ugijar. There was a small one just below the hermitage of Saint Anton at the entrance of the town and a few near the builders merchants on the Murtas road. There was a brand new enormous greenhouse on the outskirts. Plasticos are an emotive issue. They are ugly, take precious water, pollute the air and land with chemicals and scar the landscape. For hundreds of years this mountainous terrain has been terraced, small hand dug terraces planted with olives or almond trees. These terraces enhance the landscape. The crops were watered by the pure water of the Sierra Nevada mountains which gushes down the mountains in channels. The distribution of water has been fairly and carefully controlled, allowing the farmers to open the irrigation channels on their land for a certain amount of time at certain intervals. This right has been handed down through the generations and is noted in the escitura (deeds) of the property. A property might have a right to the water for two hours every week on a Monday afternoon. The farmer takes this opportunity to flood his land, soaking the earth and filling up his water tank. These water tanks are known as bolsas and double as a swimming pool in the height of summer, though they are usually rich in wildlife such as snakes so there's no way I would swim in one. This system of irrigation was introduced by the Moors and has enabled the Alpujarras to be fertile right through the dry summer months.

The plasticos are something else. Huge tracts of land are leveled. Rolling hills are massacred. The tops of the hills are blown up with explosives and this exploded earth is used to fill in the valleys between the hills, creating huge flat plateaus on which the plastic greenhouses are built. If the hills are too big to explode, the sides of the mountains are gouged out leaving ugly scars in the landscape. So hills that have lain for thousands of years are destroyed, spoiling the immediate landscape and the views from further up the mountain. The drive down from Ugijar to Berja would have been a scenic route as recently as a decade ago. Now the once picturesque valley is simply a valley of plastic.

Nobody in town like the plastics, and they don't want them here, save for the few men who make a lot of money. The water in the water channels is not flowing as freely as it used to and there are rumors that it has been diverted to the thirsty plasticos. There is talk that permission is about to be granted for another 80 new greenhouses. If this goes ahead, the beautiful, unspoiled Alpujarras will be swallowed up in a sea of plastic.

Within a week of arriving in Ugijar Rico Santos had entered my life. Rico Santos was born and bred in Ugijar. He knew everybody in town. He had all the latest gossip and spent his days in the bars collecting even more gossip. He was brought up by staunchly Catholic parents and could be found at the back of the church every Sunday. He took part in the church service but refused to partake of the bread and the wine. He also carried the saint every year at the fiesta. This was a family tradition and he was determined to carry it on until he dies.

"Emilio is not your man," he said.

I was standing in the bar next door to the bank drinking a delicious cup of coffee, the likes of which it is impossible to find anywhere in England. Which is probably a good thing as I would have a coffee addiction if I could drink coffee like this every day. Rico Santos sidled up to me and put his arm around my shoulder.

"I don't want to see you make the wrong decision Heelaree," he said in Spanish. I was already managing to understand quite a lot of the Spanish language.

"Emilio is not your man. I want to help you. I know a builder who has been building in this area for 17 years. I take you to see his work".

"How do you know my name?"

"Everybody knows your name. You are the lady who has bought the convent."

As he spoke I couldn't help but notice that the clock in the bar said 11:11. There's nothing unusual in that said my rational mind. If you have your coffee at eleven o'clock then the chances of being in the middle of a conversation at 11:11am are quite high.

Even so, I took note.

"Emilio is not a builder. He is a plumber. The job on the convent is too big for him. He doesn't understand these old buildings because he is not a local man."

Rico Santos was correct. Emilio was actually brought up in Germany.

"I have not told Emilio to start work. I have not decided who to use yet."

"I know a good builder, an expert who has studied building at college and whose father was a builder in these mountains. It is in his blood."

This was interesting. I was not searching for this builder, he was being brought to me. So I agreed to look at the property he had recently renovated in Nechite. Rico Santos drove me up the mountain in his ancient Rover, beyond Valor, higher and higher. Each time he braked, the car veered sharply to the right, bringing us close to the sheer drop over the edge of the mountain road. The gradient of the road must be at least one in two and there was no sign of a crash barrier anywhere. We pulled up outside the last house in a tiny village, so high up that I could see the Mediterranean sea glistening in the distance. The house was fantastic, a true work of art. The sink was a hand thrown bowl decorated with cobalt blue flowers. The rustic tiles had been expertly laid in a diagonal pattern and the standard of all the work was high. Outside the house, next to the village fountain, was a hand built seating area made from broken stones, typical of the area. I needed to meet the man who had created this and so he was duly summoned to the bar in Ugijar.

Miguel was young, only 26 years old. He had long dark wavy hair and was slightly built. He didn't look anything like a builder, more like an artist. I noticed his long fingered hands and I was not surprised when I found out that he played the saxophone. He also spoke a little English.

"Have you been building for long?"

"For 16 years."

He must have started at a very young age. Ten.

"My family are a family of builders and I love to build. It is in my heart."

"Which is more in your heart, your music or building?"

"I want to restore your convent. This building it is in my heart. I have fallen in love with the convent."

He was saying all the right things.

"How did you learn English?" I asked.

"First I learn in school and then I learn through the music. Bob Dylan, Lou Reed, Van Morrison."

That was it. The mention of Van Morrison clinched the deal before we had ever made the deal. Van Morrison had always been my favourite musician so, taking this as a sign, I decided there and then that he was my man. But how was I going to tell Emilio? I was going to have to ask him to move all of his stuff out of the convent.

That night as I lay in bed I couldn't get to sleep. It was the full moon. I knew I needed to tell Emilio and get that over with, so I phoned him the following morning. He was polite but curt when he heard what I had to say. "I will move my things today," he said and hung up on me.

As I entered the English bar, I was assaulted by a wall of coldness. Emilio was leaning against the bar talking to the English couple who ran it. They cast hatred in my direction. As I approach the bar Emilio turned his back to me.

"Emilio there is no problem is there? I had never given you the go ahead for the work. I only asked you to take a look."

"No. I have other work. You have the key? I will move my things."

I handed him the key. "Do you want me to give you a hand moving the stuff?"

"No. I have a friend waiting at the convent right now to help me. I will return the key when I have finished."

"I'll meet you down there in an hour you can give me the key then." I needed to keep close track of this key. An hour later the convent had been cleared. Emilio handed me the key and drove off without a word or a backward glance. As I stood there in the entrance hall holding the key, I began to cry. I could not stop the tears, they just flowed down my cheeks as I quietly sobbed. I felt like such a wimp. One hurdle and I was reduced to tears. Why did I feel like this? I knew the answer. I had nobody to talk things through with. I had no television, no phone, no internet and no friends. I hardly spoke any Spanish so I couldn't communicate very well with the locals, nor could I understand overheard snatches of conversation. My landlord had promised me a phone line and high speed internet access. These had not materialized. Phoning friends in England entailed a long walk from my apartment in Valor to a temperamental phone box at the bottom of an extremely steep hill which simply ate my money without connecting me. Drying my tears and allowing time for my nose to lose its redness, I felt brave enough to go back to the English bar.

"If you want to leave a message for Rico Santos I will not give it to him. He owes me 200 euros for beer." The woman behind the bar addressed me the moment I entered. There was nobody else in the bar. She glanced up at me and I think she could see that I had been crying. She softened slightly.

"Everybody had been depending on the work at the convent," she said. "Now they are not getting your money, they are not your friend." So money buys friendship around here, I thought to myself. I can do without friends like that.

The first hurdle to be overcome was negotiating a price for the building work with Miguel. I decided it would be better to pay him by the day rather than for the job. That way I could employ him until I ran out of money and get as much of the building done as possible. This is quite normal in Spain. He told me his daily rate was 70 euros for him and 50 euros for his assistant, which I thought was perfectly reasonable. However, shortly before he was due to start work he came to my apartment in Valor to tell me that it was actually 70 euros plus

30 for an insurance tax. For each person. That seemed quite excessive and so I decided to check this out with another Englishman was also paying his builders by the day. I was assured that this was correct and normal. Since my arrival I had been constantly reminded to be careful not to get ripped off. I was told that every foreigner who comes out to these mountains gets ripped off. The locals see the foreigners as wealthy so they have one price for the locals and a different price for foreigners. So I was being extra cautious and double checking every-thing. I decided the safest thing to do was all negotiations through the local lawyer Maria. Maria was also a good friend of Rico Santos and spoke some English. That way I knew everything would be legal and above board. I found myself in the lawyer's office with Maria, Rico Santos and the builder. Maria was going to act as translator, write any cheques and keep a written record of all transactions.

"Who is going to pay my costs?" asked Maria. Maria was sitting behind her desk in her newly built office. Her father, chief of police in the town, had built Maria this office. Above the office were two apart-ments, one for Maria and one for her father who had recently remarried. His first wife, Maria's mother , died a painful, lingering death from motor neurone disease. Piles of documents were stacked on the desk. Maria was a very large lady with deep brown rings under her eyes even though she could not have been more than 30 years old. I wondered whether her weight had anything to do with the untimely death of her mother. She was wearing a low cut strapless top and black fishnet stockings. Her tiny skirt revealed mountains of thigh and I found it difficult keeping my eyes off her legs. "Just a moment," said Maria as she typed something on her keyboard. She was clearly delighted to get a chance to show off her English.

I looked around the room. It had one small window looking out onto a small patch of garden. Her certificates and graduation photo were on display on the wall. The chairs were canvas sling back chairs that creaked loudly every time any of us moved.

"Who will pay my costs?" she repeated. She had the air of a queen addressing her subjects. The builder agreed to pay her costs and the negotiations began. Suddenly it seemed as if the price had gone up. Now the builder wanted 120 euros for himself, 100 for the assistant and 80 for the laborers. That is 300 euros a day for three men. It was explained to me that 30 euros a day for each man is a necessity for the insurance so that actually makes it 90, 70 and 50 respectively. It just seemed so excessive. But I reminded myself that the other English man had told me that this was normal. And neither the lawyer nor Rico Santos seemed the slightest bit disturbed by this price. I wished at that moment that I was not in this alone. I wished I had someone to discuss it with. But I was alone and this was my decision to take. "It is too expensive," I stated. "The 30 euros is too much."

"This is for the national insurance," Maria explained. "It has to be paid. This is a big project and they will be working on the roof. You need to have this in case one of them falls."

This didn't feel right. I had an uncomfortable feeling in my stomach but I brushed it aside. Everyone seemed to think the price was fine.

"That is my price. It is up to you. You can find someone cheaper if you want."

Maria translated the words of the builder. This seemed like such a reasonable thing to say. Surely if he was ripping me off he wouldn't have given me such an easy get out? I knew, and so did he, that there was a serious lack of decent builders available in the area. There were plenty of second class builders around but anyone half decent was booked up for months ahead. So reluctantly I agreed to the price. Smiles and handshakes all round, and a sigh of relief that we had an agreement. We had a deal.

Once outside a discussion in Spanish took place. I only spoke a bit of Spanish but I deduced that we were going for a drink at Tia's bar. Rico Santos, Miguel the builder and I headed for the bar. We got talking about astrology. Rico Santos was born on the 8th March, a Pisces like me. The eighth day of the third month. Eight plus three equals eleven.

"What year?"

"1957"

1+9+5+7=22. Double eleven.

"So it is good. Now we have agreed payment we can agree a date to start. In about three weeks." Miguel was flushed with the effects of alcohol. And the thought of all that money, no doubt. I was tired and ready to go home. They had just started on one of their legendary drinking sessions. Already Rico Santos had had half a dozen drinks. It was possible to drink for 24 hours a day in this town. I made my excuses and left them to it. 300 euros a day I was going to be paying. I just hoped they were fast workers.

CHAPTER SIX

Soon I was settling in to the Spanish way of life. Each morning as I drove the short distance down the mountain from Valor to Ugijar, I had to pinch myself. Was I really living here in these beautiful hills? My heart sang along with the Spanish music on the car radio. One morning, about four weeks after I had arrived in Spain, I was sitting alone on the terrace of a bar in the main road drinking coffee. I noticed an elegant, slim, white haired man walk past. He looked like a male version of my mother who is also elegant, slim and white-haired. I wondered who he was as he did not look like a local man. This man stood out as being different. I did not have to wait long to find out. Later that day I was walking down towards the convent when I saw him again. He was walking up the road towards me and our paths crossed at the door of the convent.

"Hello," he said. So he spoke English. Most of the locals didn't.

"I hear you have bought the convent." In a town of this size it was not possible to have secrets.

"Then I must give you the book that my family has. It is the book of your house for it is a very ancient place and in this book is recorded the names of the people that lived there. You know it was home to the Knights Templars?"

I felt like I had been punched in the stomach.

"I thought it was an old convent."

"In the middle of the seventeenth century it was indeed a convent. But in the early 1500s it was a Franciscan friary. And before that it was home to the Knights Templars. I have it written in the book, which my sister has. There are written in here the names of the Knights. Only this part was for the Knights. The other two thirds of the property is more recent. You have bought the oldest part. I know a lot about the house because I was born in it. My family used to own all of it, even the church. I was born in this house."

So the convent was much older than I had thought. I knew it dated back to the sixteenth century but the Templars were around in the twelfth and thirteenth centuries. And the Knights Templars were in Ugijar? I was both thrilled and a little spooked by this information.

"Would you like to have a look inside?"

"No, I don't think so," he said. "I think I will get romantic." I think he meant nostalgic. At least I hoped he did.

"Come on," I encouraged. "I'd love to hear more of the history of the convent. What's your name?"

"I am Gabriel," he replied. What an appropriate name for a person born in a convent.

He followed me through the door.

"Ah, this door it is from the thirteenth century," he pointed towards the carved door. "It is very old." I silently wondered whether it was his family who had varnished it with that ghastly yellow varnish.

"Did you know that it was once a school of boarding for children, and the nuns in the convent looked after the children." Gabriel's English was not perfect. He had taught himself to speak English as a young man, using BBC LP's which he played on an old wind up gramophone, sitting under the tree by the hermitage.

Gabriel was a beautiful looking man. He was a businessman who now lived and worked in the north of Spain. He came back to Ugijar fairly frequently as he owned several properties in the town. He had lost his much loved wife to cancer five years earlier and carried the grief of this loss tangibly. The love of his life has gone and left a gaping hole. He was an emotional man and decided he did not want to be in the convent because it was difficult for him to see it in such a bad state, so our visit was very brief. He left me with a kiss on each cheek and a mind full of wonder. I could hardly believe it. I owned a part of Templar history. The next day I bumped into Gabriel again. He was standing in the internet café eating tapas and drinking wine. His face lit up as I approached.

"You like tapas?" asked Gabriel as I walked towards him. He ordered me a grape juice, which comes with a slice of freshly made tortilla, an onion and potato omelette.

"The word tapas means gift," he told me. "The Alpujarras is the last place in Spain where tapas is given free of charge. Now since my wife has died I do not cook, I do not eat at my home, I am eating always Tapas in the bars."

He obviously did not eat too much of it, his figure was slim and youthful. We sat down together and he began to open up to me.

"I had a girlfriend for one year, one year only." he told me. "I do not want to marry again. I was married for 35 years. Here in the Alpujarras when we marry, we marry for life." A sadness engulfed him momentarily like a dark blanket and I saw his eyes moisten.

"Do you like to dance?" he asked me, recovering his composure.

"Yes, to the right music I like to dance."

"I like to dance. I like to dance Spanish dancing." His eyes came alive at the mention of dancing.

"Oh, show me some Spanish dancing!" I exclaimed.

The Spanish music was playing on the stereo in the bar. The bar was owned by a Spanish speaking South American and she loved varied styles of music.

"I like to dance to this music, this real Spanish music." He leant towards me and spoke intently.

"Show me," I repeated.

"No, no." He shook his head. "I cannot do this until I have been drinking a few more wines. Do you like to dance?"

"Oh yes, but I only like to dance to music that makes me feel like dancing. Like Van Morrison."

As I uttered these words the Spanish song ended and I heard the familiar sound of the voice of Van Morrison. A Van Morrison track playing in this small internet café half way up a mountain. What timing!

"This is Van Morrison!" I exclaimed in delight. "This is my favorite music to dance to."

"Show me how you dance."

"Well I don't dance in Spanish style, I dance in a rather free way."

"Show me, show me, show me," he demanded.

The bar was empty except for Gabriel, an old man and myself.

So I showed him a bit of my dancing, wild and free it is. He watched me intently and then I noticed a certain look on his face. He looked directly into my eyes.

"Would you like to come to the sea with me tomorrow?" he whispered. "I would like to show you the sea."

"Oh. Tomorrow no. No, thank you." I had seen that look in his eyes. He was a lovely man but he was a good 30 years older than me and I was not looking for a relationship. The trouble with a small town is that it was impossible to avoid people and two days later I bumped into Gabriel again. He was delighted to see me and he beamed.

"Let me take you to a good tapas bar."

Gabriel took me by the arm and gently guided me across the square. We walked a few hundred yards to a tiny bar. It was empty, except for a middle aged woman sitting behind the bar watching a Spanish soap on a television high up in the corner of the room.

Here our drinks were accompanied by a plate of the most exquisite vegetarian risotto I have ever tasted. It was bright yellow. Chick peas, beans, onions and garlic and sprinkled chopped fresh herbs.

"This," Gabriel told me, "is traditional Alpujarran cooking. This is prepared with love. This is the food that the wife has prepared for the family. Anyone coming to the bar is offered a small portion."

When we finished our drink he took me to another bar. "What tapas would you like? Here you have a choice of fish, ham, cheese, meats, egg."

"I would like egg please."

When my egg arrived it came in a fresh white bread roll with a handful of whole toasted, salted almonds on the side.

"The almonds are grown on trees less than one kilometer from here," Gabriel told me.

When his tapas arrived I was astounded. Fresh crusty bread coated with mayonnaise on which was laid a thick slice of smoked salmon.

With each drink came more tapas. "I will have cheese please". I expected a slice of cheese with a piece of bread. Instead I was presented with another white roll, this time brushed with olive oil, crushed fresh tomatoes and garlic. Inside was a hot, thick, toasted slice of goat's cheese. It was served with a small portion of hand cut chips fried in olive oil. Delicious! I could see why Gabriel lived on tapas.

The more Gabriel drank, the wider his smile became.

"Hilary, Hilary," he whispered, " I can dance for you now."

He backed into a doorway leading to the adjoining restaurant where he could only be seen by me, and there he began to dance. The dance was in every atom of his being. He stamped his feet. He clapped his hands above his head. His hips moved in perfect harmony with the music. His face took on an expression of bliss. There was no doubt that he was an exceptional dancer, but I was a bit embarrassed by this private performance. He was dancing just for me.

"Yes Gabriel, that is very good but I must go now. It is late."

"Yes come. We will go."

Walking back to the car he suddenly became very passionate.

"I am so glad to have met you. We will take things slowly yes. There is no hurry."

"Gabriel, I am quite happy to have you as a friend but just as a friend."

"Yes, I want to spend lots of time with you."

"Gabriel, I am not looking for a relationship. "

"Yes but I want to take you lots of places and I will show you lots of things here in Spain. I am not going to be going up north on business. I am going to stay here and live in Ugijar."

Alarm bells began to ring in my head. "Gabriel, I like you as a friend but I am not interested in anything else."

As we reached my car he pulled me towards him. I pulled back sharply. I did not want this. I did not want a boyfriend.

"I have to go. I will see you tomorrow."

I leaped into the safety of my car and drove off. Phew! These Spanish men were passionate people.

I was looking for the signs but I couldn't find any. It was as if I had been led to this place and then abandoned. The 11 11 had not appeared for weeks. I felt really alone and lost.

As usual, I spent time each day in meditation, 20 minutes in the morning before I started my day and the same at the end of the day. I simply sat with my eyes closed, upright and relaxed, focusing on my breathing and asking to be guided. This, I believe, is the simple way of creating coincidences in my life. I try and keep my inner gaze focused on the point on my forehead between my eyebrows but my focus on this day was not good.

"Why have the signs stopped?" my mind kept saying. "Just when I need them the most they've gone." Niggling doubts began to creep into my consciousness. Maybe this was a stupid thing to do. Giving up my settled life in England for a life up here in this small, isolated town half way up a mountain.

It is not always possible to keep the mind clear and focused. Some days are easier than others. Today was one of those days when my thoughts were like a chattering monkey.

My neck was becoming a real problem. It had started causing me problems when I got the key back from Emilio, that day when I cried in the convent. It had suddenly become locked and I could hardly turn my head. I had been hoping that it would gradually ease off but it was getting worse. I was in constant pain and was having to take painkillers to get through the day. I needed to find a good masseur. Where would I find a masseur in this area? I decided I needed to get out into the sunshine and I wandered down past the convent towards the square. As I turned up the road I passed the shop owned by the German man. That looked like an interesting shop. It was even more interesting when I entered, for there sitting behind the counter was a woman with a familiar face.

"Hello, can I help you?" she asked in English. I must look English. I DO look English! I was looking at this woman quite intently trying to work out who she was.

"You look really familiar. Where have I seen you before?" I asked.

"I don't know."

"Do I look familiar to you?"

"Vaguely familiar. I think I've seen you before but I'm not sure where."

I racked my brain. I knew this woman. I was certain of that. I think I had seen her quite a long time ago. Then suddenly it clicked into place.

"Gaunts House!" I exclaimed. "Do you have a connection with Gaunts House?" Gaunts House is a spiritual community deep in the Dorset countryside. For many years I would spend a week in the summer helping out at the summer festival. This is where I had seen her.

"I certainly did. I spent several years at Gaunts house."

"Well, I used to be a volunteer at the summer gathering. So that's where I have seen you. You're Claire, aren't you?"

"Yes," she replied. " I remember you now."

This was a sign. Meeting someone from Dorset up here in Ugijar is remarkable.

"What are you doing up here?" I asked.

"I'm setting up a retreat center high in the mountains. What about you?"

"I'm setting up a yoga center here in Ugijar. In the old ruined convent around the corner."

"Wow, that's a big job you've taken on," she noted.

"Yes I know. But I've found a builder and work should start in a couple of weeks. And guess what? It used to be a Knights Templar church."

Dorset, which is the county in England where I had first met Claire, was the place where I first knowingly came across a Templar church. I was with Anthony at the time, on one of our regular jaunts out into the beautiful English countryside. We loved walking along country lanes lined with hedgerows and visiting old churches, which we usually found unlocked. We would go inside and spend time just sitting quietly soaking up the silence. We both lived in the center of Bournemouth, a conurbation where it was difficult to find silence.

One day we had a day which I call the 'fifteen day'. It was the fifteenth of May and beautiful weather so we had decided to drive further than we usually drove. We drove beyond a country town called Dorchester and took a turning off the main road, looking for somewhere quiet we could walk. The sun was already quite low in the sky. The road was quite steep, going downhill into a basin rather like a miniature version of the basin that Ugijar sits in. At the bottom of the hill was a tiny church adjacent to a farm. I looked at my watch. 1551, just past ten to four. The 11:11 day which we had experienced a few months earlier was still in my mind so I looked at the trip meter. 15. We had filled up the petrol tank just before Dorchester. So it was no surprise to me to see that the milometer was 115115. Getting out the car we noticed a line of people walking along the ridge of the hill. "That looks like a rambling society," I pointed them out to Anthony. I counted them. 15. I counted them again. Yes, I was right. There were fifteen people walking along the ridge.

As we walked towards the church, a flock of birds swooped down towards us as if they were giving us a personal fly past. I counted them; fifteen birds.

I knew before I entered that the bible was going to be open at chapter fifteen. Sure enough, it was open at Revelations 15.

'Seven angels with seven plagues came out of heaven.'

Not fifteen angels? Too obscure for me that message. Was the number seven relevant? Is that what it means? I picked up the booklet about the history of the church and on the front was a photograph of an old stone carving. It showed Mary Magdalene anointing the foot of Jesus and it dated back to the twelfth century. It said that the church was Knights Templar and that this carving dated from that period of history. It was a small fragment of what must once have been a much larger carving, but it filled me with wonder.

"You must come up and see where I am living and take a look at the center," said Claire. "Have you got a car?"

I was indeed now the owner of a huge, ancient Seat Toledo, which Rico Santos had found for me. It still smelt of the previous owner who had an issue with body odor, but at least it was reliable. It started first time, throwing huge plumes of black smoke into the atmosphere as it burst into life. It was a bit embarrassing but there wasn't a huge choice of second hand cars in the area.

We agreed to meet in a few days and Claire recommended the masseur who advertised in English on the notice board in the shop. What a stroke of luck. An English masseur living in a nearby village. Even better was the fact that his partner, like me, was an astrologer. Things were looking up.

On my way back to the car I called in at a bar to get my coffee fix. My newly acquired addiction to coffee was so strong that I was prepared to go into a bar and drink it alone, despite the stares I was subjected to by the mainly male clientele. As I dangled from the edge of a high bar stool I became aware of a pair of eyes boring into me. I looked across and saw an elderly man sitting at the far corner of the bar. He beckoned me over. I ignored him. So he called out something in Spanish and beckoned me again.

"Hey. You own the convent. Yes?"

"Yes. Why?"

"Come."

This time when he beckoned me I went. He pulled a paper serviette from the box on the bar and called to the bartender for a pen. He was old and fat, his cotton shirt fastened around his big belly by the only two buttons that could meet. His chest was hairy and he wore a heavy gold chain. He was obviously a 'gitano' as the gypsies are known. I was sure I recognized him as one of the street sweepers. He normally pushed a dustcart with his wife and daughter. Once I had walked over to put some rubbish in the bin by the square.

"No, no," I was told by my Spanish companion. "You must throw it on the floor or the gitanos won't have any work to do."

The old man grabbed me firmly by the wrist and pulled me closer. Then he slowly started to draw on the serviette. It looked like a rose arbor. He pointed to the ground and then pointed to his drawing and I thought he was trying to tell me that the convent used to have a garden. I racked my brains for the Spanish word for garden.

"Jardin?"

"No, no."

He tried again, this time making it into a longer rose arbor. I didn't understand what he was trying to tell me. He pointed to the ground. What else grows on arbors I wondered. Grapes? Beans? I shook my head. It was no use. My lack of Spanish was a huge barrier to communication. I could sense his frustration. He took the paper from me and continued to draw. This time he drew a church with a tower next to the arbor. His dark brown, bloodshot, watery eyes penetrated mine, as if he could get the message across to me telepathically. He squeezed my upper arm and shook it, peering intensely into my eyes. I tried hard to understand.

A church garden? A church with a rose arbor as its approach? A covered walkway?

Then all of a sudden I understood. The penny had dropped. "A tunnel!"

My face instantly showed my delight and the old man thumped bar with glee at having succeeded in getting his message across. Then he tapped the side of his nose with his finger. It's obviously a secret. He was telling me of the rumor of a secret tunnel between the convent and the church.

Having succeeded in his mission of giving me this message, this nugget of information, he screwed up the piece of paper and dropped it on the floor, where it joined the piles of cigarette ends, tissues, sugar wrappers, cigarette boxes and various other debris.

CHAPTER SEVEN

I was lying on my yoga mat on the terrace by the pool, under an old olive tree. One of the main attractions of renting this particular apartment in Valor was the private saltwater swimming pool. Unfortunately the water was not heated and the pool did not have a cover so I could not swim. But I still loved to do my yoga by the pool, watching as the swallows dived sharply down towards the water, feeding on the wing. As I sat cross-legged and prepared for my yoga, I looked around. The water of the pool was reflected in the olive tree, shimmering light reflected on the brittle leaves. The tree was dry and wizened and it reminded me of the people, dark skinned and lined where the sun had dried their skin, just like the shriveled, wrinkly olives. The unpicked olives lay on the terrace where they had fallen. I looked down at my bare legs and already I could see my skin starting to dry up in the still strong November sun, so I picked up an olive and squeezed the rich oil onto my skin. All I could hear was the singing of the birds. The oranges on the orange trees were almost ripe and I was looking forward to picking them. The mandarins were still green and would be much later to ripen, probably at Christmas time. The lemon tree had one yellow lemon, which had raced ahead of its siblings, which were still green. The pomegranates were almost over. The few remaining ones had burst open and the birds had feasted on the juicy insides. There were no figs on the fig tree, the second crop of the year had been and gone. Figs were introduced to Spain by the Arabs and the local shops sold figs stuffed with almonds which are nutritious and tasty. Nature was abundant around here and I could imagine how little this had changed over the years.

The abundance of nature helped to make this place so special. I wondered if it had something to do with the purity of the air. At night the skies were a lacework of stars. I had never seen so many stars in the sky. There was so little light pollution in this area that there was a major observatory not so far away. I was so used to the orange glow of city skies that it was as if I was a child seeing the real sky for the first time. Sometimes I just stood in the garden at night, staring up at the skies for hours, and I marveled at the sight of all those sparkling, twinkling stars. If I was lucky I would see shooting stars.

A few days after my initial meeting with Claire I drove down to Ugijar to meet her in the shop where she worked. I was really looking forward to her company. The shop belonged to a German man who had lived in the area for many years and Claire helped him out now and then. As we sat chatting someone in a hat entered.

"Hello Claire." He came over and greeted her with a kiss.

"Hello Marcus. Let me introduce you to Hilary. She has bought the old convent around the corner and has only been living here for a few weeks."

Marcus shook my hand. "This is Marcus who does the massage," explained Claire.

This was just the person I needed to meet. "I was going to ring you. I need some help with my neck. I don't know what's happened to it. I can hardly move my head and it's really painful."

Marcus put his hands on my shoulders and felt around the area. "The whole area feels pretty tight. Why don't you come over to my place tomorrow and I'll take a proper look at it? My partner is down at the internet café in the square. If you go down there she'll draw you a map of how to get to our place. I'll join you in a minute."

The internet café is the only place in town where I can check my emails, so I know the internet café well. I had never met Marcus's partner before but somehow, as soon as I walked in, I knew it must be her. She was sitting at a table with a middle aged couple.

"Are you Marcus's partner?" I asked.

"Yes, I'm Nicky. Sit down sweetheart, come and join us. This is Tim and Julia. They live in the same village as Marcus and I."

I recognized the name of this village. It was just a few kilometers up from Cherin.

"I understand you're an astrologer."

"Yes I am," replied Nicky and her face lit up as faces do when one astrologer meets another. Astrology is a language all of its own, a language that cuts through cultural boundaries and the restrictions of spoken words. The symbols of astrology can be understood without words. If I hand an astrology chart to a French, German, Finnish, Italian or Greek astrologer... whatever their native language, they can read the astrology chart. It's a language of symbols and it's not that widely spoken. So to meet an astrologer out here in Ugijar was an absolute delight.

"This is Tim who is a history teacher and Julia his wife."

Tim was dressed in an outfit from the 1930s. He was wearing three quarter length tweed breeches with long socks and ankle boots and he was carrying a long wooden staff. Echoes from the past.

"Is it you who bought the convent?"

I nodded.

"I'd love to have a look inside. I'm very interested in history. What are you going to do with it?"

"I'm going to set up a yoga center. I've got a builder and he's due to start work any time now. If you want to have a look at the place you can. I've got the key on me."

"Let's wait for Marcus and we can all go down and have a look," Nicky suggested.

Half an hour later we all entered the convent. I could see by their faces that they were shocked by the state of it. Then Tim spotted the door.

"Ah, the symbol of the House of Hanover. That must be eighteenth century," he remarked.

"No I think it's older than that. I have been told it's thirteenth century."

"Definitely not. The House of Hanover covers the period 1714 to 1917 so it's not that old."

"But look at the carving. It's a double headed eagle which is the symbol of the Templars."

"No. That's a sign of the House of Hanover. Besides which it couldn't possibly be a Templar place. The Templars were never here in this part of Spain. In the twelfth and thirteenth century, this place was occupied by the Moors. They were here from about 700AD until the middle of the sixteenth century."

I was disappointed. Was he right? I had thought that this door was a link to the Templars. I was sure that a double-headed eagle was a Templar sign.

I was confused now. He was a history teacher so he must know his history. I made a mental note to do some research on the internet. What I didn't realize at this point was that he was a history teacher who had been conditioned to tell history as the establishment wanted it to be told. The real history still lived on in this town through legends and through the memories of the local people.

When I saw Gabriel later that day I told him what Tim had said. He was furious.

"I do not lie. My family we have been living in this place for many years. We have the book of the history of the house and there we have it written. The Knights Templars."

"Are you sure it says Knights Templars? Maybe it says Knights Hospitalers?"

"NO." Gabriel shouted. "Do you think I cannot read? It is written in the book and it is written their names as well."

"I really want to see this book. Can I have a look at it?"

"Yes, I tell my sister and she will bring the book when she is coming next to Ugijar. Then you can see. I like that you meet my sister. I like to introduce you to her. We can all go and eat tapas together." His voice was softer. I'd rather just see the book without the tapas. But I would do whatever was necessary to see it, within reason.

CHAPTER EIGHT

It was time for my first massage with Marcus and I headed off to Picena. This village was jokingly referred to by the English people in the area as the council estate of the Alpujarras. I had gradually connected with some English people in the area because people from quite a wide radius would come to Ugijar to use the internet café. There were dozens of small, whitewashed villages in this mountain range, each with their own character and individual quirks. Picena was particularly behind the times, though it was about to be brought sharply into the 21st century. Firstly the road to the next village, Cherin, had been improved making access to these once remote villages easier, and secondly because a massive new road was soon to be built right across the upper valley of the Alpujarras, scarring the erstwhile natural terrain and gouging open the whole valley. Already tourist buses could be seen once a week, carrying holiday makers from the rapidly expanding coastal resorts such as Roquetas de Mar and Almerimar, the huge coaches trying to negotiate the hair pin bends on these narrow mountain roads. A massive development of new houses was being built higher up the hill overlooking the village of Picena by a developer from down by the coast. They were terraced and had their own garages and were being marketed at second home owners, especially the English. The villagers were not happy about this intrusion but they were not too worried either. Rumor had it that the houses had been built on a water table which all the people living locally knew about, but the developers didn't. So everyone was quite sure that the new houses would fall down in a few years then things would return to the status quo.

Marcus and Nicky's house was most definitely not twentieth century. It was a tiny terraced cottage built into the side of the hill on the far edge of the village, constructed from local materials and at a guess it was at least a few hundred years old. I had to walk down a very steep hill to reach their front door. I was greeted by the local dog population, with the whole valley echoing to the furious barking of 20 dogs. Half of them looked wild and I wondered if any of them were rabid. I avoided eye contact. That had seemed to work when I was followed by dogs in the gypsy area of Ugijar and thankfully I reached Marcus and Nicky's cottage unscathed. Their front door opened and I was greeted by more barking. Marcus and Nicky had adopted four of the local strays. Their front door opened onto the top floor of the house and the back door opened on the ground floor. The bathroom was in the basement, as if it was an afterthought. I could imagine somebody had just gone down into the basement with a shovel and dug out this extra room, like they did in the cave houses on the other side of the Sierra Nevada mountains. The walls of the house were earth and the ceilings were wood and cane, the same as the convent. The width of each of the rooms was dictated by the length of the beams, just like in the convent. There must have been a lack of tall trees around here because the entire house was only about two meters wide. There was a tiny winding staircase with huge steps going down to the first bedroom, which in turn led down to the second bedroom. Stairs from here led down to the bathroom. The wooden beams were riddled with termites but as it was only rented, they were not too worried. The whole house was heated by an open fire and a tiny wood stove, the wood gathered from the surrounding hills. It was November and the weather was quite cold today. The wood stove had been lit in preparation for my massage so the living room was thick with smoke.

As I lay down on the couch in the tiny narrow living room, which was also the kitchen and the dining room, Marcus began to work on my neck. It was such a relief after all these weeks of pain to get some massage. It was not just my neck troubling me. It was my left hip too. "They're linked," Marcus told me. "As I release your neck your hip will release too."

He started with a full body massage and didn't reach my neck until almost the end of the session. "I reckon I can fix things but it'll take six sessions."

"That's fine," I replied. I knew I couldn't carry on taking painkillers for much longer.

"I'll give you some cranio sacral therapy in the next session."

Anthony had studied cranio sacral therapy when he was living in Sussex. It turned out they had trained with the same guy. I was pleased by the coincidence, though I still had not seen 11:11 appearing for a while.

There were two roads back to Valor from Picena, the high road and the low road. I took the high road and drove beyond Valor to the natural springs. There was a steep, narrow track that led down into a valley. It was a dead end. At the end of the track was a small cave with six or seven natural springs each of which had a completely different taste. One outlet was naturally sparkling, another was almost red with the iron content, another had a lesser iron content. My favorite was the one that flowed about 20 meters away from the main springs. This was water how nature intended it to be. Pure, soft, clear, cool and refreshing. There were other springs in the area, each with its own qualities, which were well known by the locals. There was a spring for healing problems with the eyes and another for digestive problems. I filled up my water bottles from my favorite spring to take back to the apartment. As I drove away from the springs, a huge snake slithered across my path. This was the first time I had seen a snake up here and I was shocked at the size of it.

'What does a snake represent?' Anthony's voice came into my head.

'Wisdom,' came the instant answer.

I was on my way to the internet café to look up some information about the double headed eagle. I went onto the Google search engine and typed 'eagle double headed' to see what came up. I wanted to know if this was connected to the Knights Templar or not. I clicked on the first site on the list:'The Double Headed Eagle of Lagash'.

The site came up on my screen, complete with background music. I was struck by the fact that it was exactly the same as the music on my kundalini yoga tape.

THE DOUBLE HEADED EAGLE OF LAGASH

Long used as the insigne of a Scottish Rite Mason, the "Double Headed Eagle of Lagash" is now the accepted emblem in the United States of America of the 32 Degree. It is the oldest crest in the world. It was a symbol of power more than two thousand years before the building of King Solomon's Temple. No other heraldic bearing, no other emblematic device of today can boast such antiquity. There seem to be some who believe that the double-headed eagle may have been a Masonic symbol as early as the twelfth century, but it probably was first known to Freemasonry in 1758.

No specific mention of the House of Hanover so I changed my search to 'double headed eagle Knights Templar'. And there it was. The same double headed eagle that had been carved into the door of the convent. Not only was it an ancient symbol of the Knights Templars, it was also well known in modern Freemasonary.

I also noticed a reference to John the Baptist and the fact that the Templars supposedly had his head and worshipped it. I found that very hard to believe, but I remembered being in the Knights Templar church in Dorset and being led to a reference to John the Baptist in the bible. I also remembered that it was Matthew Chapter 11, verse 11. Could John the Baptist be connected to the 11:11 in some way?

CHAPTER NINE

Work had started on the convent in earnest. I walked down into town to have a look. Despite having told me that he would be working on his own to start with, Miguel my musical builder had brought three other men along. The place was a scene of chaos and destruction. Already all the ceilings on the first floor were down and they had started dismantling the roof, exposing the first floor of the convent to the open air. Firstly I asked Miguel about his decision to employ another three men.

"Mas rapido," I was told, it's quicker. "Just to start with. You happy, yes?"

I nodded because maybe he was right. But I noticed that in their enthusiasm they had been careless. Several of the original windows had been broken.

"Look you need to be careful. I want to use all the original old doors and windows. You need to take them off their hinges and put them somewhere safe."

He agreed to do this. "And I want to save all the roof tiles".

My plan was to have a large roof terrace for outdoor yoga, as the courtyard was not big enough. The roof tiles were beautiful, individual, hand made terracotta. Spare tiles like this would not be easy to get hold of. The whole roof was being taken down. Completely. I questioned whether that was absolutely necessary and Miguel explained that a new ring beam had to be put on top of the earth walls, which could take the weight of the new terrace. The old walls were at least a meter thick and were made of earth and stones. On top of these a brick and cement wall would have to be built, reinforced from the inside with metal. Then reinforced concrete beams would be laid between the walls, which would be strong enough to take the concrete for the terrace.

As the roof tiles were being taken off, all the original wooden beams, dozens of them, were revealed. They were hand cut chestnut beams, some over six meters long. I wondered who laid them there. Was it the Franciscans? Or the Templars? They were bound with the type of rough string that I remembered from my childhood. Some were still in perfect condition. Bound in string with intricate knots tied to locally grown cane. They were nailed together with massive old-fashioned metal nails. They were in surprisingly good condition considering the overall state of the convent. Some of the walls were faced with small, Moorish terracotta bricks. Some were a mixture of stone and brick. Wooden beams were laid on the main walls, the width of the rooms being dictated by the length of the beams. Some beams were sound but others were rotten at the ends where they had been exposed to water.

The amount of debris being created by the walls that support the roof was enormous as the walls were so thick. Earth and rubble was being taken away to the local dump by a small dumper truck. This method of working left something to be desired because whilst the dumper truck was away at the dump the others sat and waited for it to come back. Twenty minutes later it would return to be filled up and off it went again. Another twenty minutes wait. And so it went on. I pointed out this state of affairs to Miguel. I was told not to worry because the rubbish should be cleared in a day or two and then they would not have to wait around.

"Come see," Miguel enthused, taking me by the hand. He pulled me towards the courtyard, his delicate long fingers holding my hand firmly.

"Look!" He pointed. There in the corner the old fountain had been revealed. I had imagined it to be round but it was rectangular, just like some of the old fountains with healing properties that I had found in the surrounding countryside. It had been built against a wall and there was a large hole where somebody had removed the water outlet. I could see the water pipe half hidden by earth and stones. It looked like lead. It was a large fountain, a 'fuente' and was built like the tower with narrow red bricks.

"We take away the trees and find this," Miguel said triumphantly.

It crossed my mind that it might have once been a spring, a natural source of fresh water. I loved the fuente, and imagined what it would look and sound like when it was flowing again. Maybe I could use the word fountain in the name of the yoga center. I would need to choose a name, maybe The Fountain Center? or the Ancient Key Center? or Ancient Lights because it has ancient lights in the escitura? or maybe The Fountain of Light?

Now that the convent was being cleared I felt brave enough to venture further, beyond the courtyard. Somehow the presence of four or five strong male builders was enough to give me the confidence I needed to enter that back room. Stooping to avoid banging my head on the low threshold, I stepped gingerly through a small doorway into the part of the convent I had not yet seen. I got a shock when I saw how huge the back section was. It must have been at least 20 meters by six meters with a high ceiling and an earth floor, just like the front section. A modern concrete beam had been put across the center, supported by a wooden pillar. Without this it is obvious that the first floor would have collapsed onto the ground floor because the back part of the convent was in much worse condition. There were old suitcases hanging from the ceiling on metal hooks that looked as if they dated back to the 1920s. In the alcove, old bottles sat on the simple wooden shelves. Set against the wall there was something that looked like a large square altar with a drainage channel and a spout on the side. It was obviously very old and made of stone.

I called Miguel. "What's this?" I asked, pointing to the altar. "What would this have been used for?"

"This is a slaughter block for killing pigs," he said. "The nuns would have kept animals here and when they kill them they keep all the parts including the blood. That is why there is the spout on the side."

"And these?" I asked pointing to two huge metal barrels.

"The nuns made all their own olive oil. They once had much land and grew all of their own food." Not any more. The convent had no garden at all now.

Despite the vast size of the place I felt claustrophobic. I had a feeling of being trapped. I had a crushing sensation on my chest, making breathing difficult. Maybe it was the dust?

There was a huge studded wooden door leaning against the wall, complete with its frame. I wondered why it was there and where it came from. There were also two pillars to which a small platform had been attached.

Later that evening I was sitting in the apartment looking at the floor plans on the deeds of the convent and trying to compare them to what I had seen earlier in the day. On the deeds, the rear section was in three parts, not two. It showed a wide room, a narrower room and then a long corridor. I had not seen a corridor earlier that day. I was sure that it had not been there. Why not? I needed to go back tomorrow and see if I had somehow missed a doorway.

The next morning I set off to check out the location of the missing corridor. I had the escitura with me, detailing the floor plans of the convent. Only two people were working that day, stacking up the unbroken roof tiles in the courtyard. I must have lost a third of them through breakage. Heading straight for the back room, I checked out the floor plan. It was undeniable. There was a complete corridor missing, and there was no sign of a doorway where the corridor should be. Not even a trace of a doorway. Why was it missing? Had the neighbor stolen it from me? I decided I would have to check it out so I went around the block to the adjoining property.

My neighbors property adjoined the other wall of the museum and was in much better condition than mine. Their door was a huge arched double doorway which opened directly onto a courtyard. I introduced myself and I was invited in to have a look around.

Their place was massive, a myriad of interconnecting rooms. They too had a fountain, but theirs was complete with running water. I worked out which was the room that adjoined the back of the convent but I could see no evidence of a stolen corridor.

"We have many books from the convent here," my neighbor told me. "This used to be part of the University of Granada."

That was news to me. I wondered if I had understood properly. "I didn't know that. That's fascinating. I love finding out about the history of the convent."

"Then you need to speak to the priest. He has a book all about the history of the church."

Did he know about the secret tunnel too? I kept silent about the tunnel.

"And you know of the painting?"

"No. What painting?" I asked.

"In the church there is a painting, very old. My front door is on this painting. And in the church they have a book about the history of Ugijar."

I made a mental note to check out this information and to try and get into the museum. On my way out I saw on the museum door it was open on Saturday mornings, so I would have to wait a few days.

I wondered what was in that missing corridor. I wondered whether there really was a tunnel. I wondered about the painting. I also wondered how long it would be before my neck stopped hurting. The constant nagging pain was something I could do without.

CHAPTER TEN

Every time I stepped out of the door of my rented apartment in Valor I didn't know what to expect. Some evenings when I stepped outside, the hill opposite glowed brilliant red. Only for a few moments and then it would change color. Some moments would make me gasp in awe at the beauty of this place. Those moments brought me right into the here and now. Each time I looked across the valley to the distant hills I had a different view, as the shadows and light created a moving, ever changing palette of colors. I loved the way the light played with the hills and the valleys, and the cloud formations were unique to this area, formations I had never seen before. It was something to do with the fact that we were 900 meters above sea level yet less than 50 kilometers from the sea. These mountains are steep and the roads were narrow and twisting. They were riddled with hairpin bends but there was a distinct lack of crash barriers. Sometimes cars went over the edge and people got killed. "They were not driving carefully enough," the locals said, "so what do they expect?"

Some days the clouds would hang below in the valley and I would be above the level of the clouds in the sun, whilst below in the valley it can be raining. Then I was reminded of the altitude. When I first arrived I used to get dizzy spells. It took me weeks to realize that these were caused by the altitude. Now I was used to it and I was not feeling dizzy any more so my body must have got accustomed to the height. I wondered if my lungs have grown bigger. Apparently this is why athletes train at high altitude. The lungs increase in size to allow the body to take in enough oxygen. Despite all the difficulties such as substandard living accommodation, I loved being up this mountain.

The last time I had driven down to the coast I had not seen another car for fifteen minutes. I had the freedom of the road. I loved it. Driving through the high valleys with the snow capped mountains in the distance, Vivaldi playing on my car CD player and not another person in sight. I was almost at the town of Berja before I saw another car.

My massage sessions were going well. Marcus started with the full body massage and followed that up with cranio sacral therapy, concentrating on the part of my neck and head where it was locked. It seemed as if there were buried memories in my muscles, long forgotten experiences, all unpleasant. No wonder I had chosen to forget them. For the first few sessions, the memories were of accidents, traumas and pain that I had experienced earlier in my life, going right back to childhood. I remembered falling from a slide in the park and landing on the concrete below and falling head first from a swing, again onto concrete. These were the days before rubberized flooring in children's play parks.

As his strong, male fingers worked into the resistant muscles on the edge of my skull, he always seemed to find a particularly painful muscle. Then he would hold his finger firmly into the muscle, pressing it until I relaxed into his touch. It was almost as if we were meditating together. Whilst the muscle was resistant, I realized I was thinking about something that had happened in my past, usually something traumatic. I would have the thought, then relax into the muscle and he would move onto another muscle and another buried memory.

The deepest memory of this life that came up was a very painful memory of an operation I had had when I was a teenager. Of course I remembered that I had had an operation but what I had not remembered was the immense terror and fear around the whole incident. Through working on my neck Marcus brought the memories I had 'stuffed' back into consciousness. These were the memories that had been so painful that I hadn't been able to allow them to remain conscious.

I'd never had a general anaesthetic before. In fact I had never even been in a hospital. I remembered crying with fear as I was prepared for the operating theatre. I was all on my own, nobody to hold my hand or support me. I was simply on a conveyor belt of patients, a number on a list, and another operation to be done. The fact that I was alone, full of fear and barely eighteen years old was irrelevant. The staff had a job to do and they were getting on with it. I was crying as I was put under and the sound of clanging bells ringing inside my head as the anaesthetic entered my body was followed by dreadful nightmares. I woke from the operation, vomited and then fainted when I tried to get up. What a dreadful experience that was!

At the end of this process of thoughts, Marcus let out a sharp shout, and flung his arm away as though he was removing something. This must be the chi massage technique that he had mentioned in his advertising leaflet. It was almost as if subconsciously he knew that something was being released. There in the muscles of my neck was held all the pain around that whole scenario. It hurt. I didn't want to keep that memory. What I didn't understand was how Marcus knew that I had just released a hidden memory. Then on the last but one session, Marcus did quite a lot of work on my arm before moving up to my neck. It was then that something different happened. I remembered a past life.

I was a monk, a man of God, bent forward across a low wall with my hands tied behind my back. I was praying with an intensity I have never experienced before, begging God to intervene and stop the slaughter of His servants. I had incredible faith that my prayers would be answered. As I looked to my left I could see my brothers, my comrades, being beheaded one by one with a huge sword. These were the monks that I had been living and praying with for many years. I think I was in charge of them in some way. Had I been responsible for converting them to Christianity or was it somehow my fault that they had been caught and now found themselves in this position, being beheaded? I was aware of feeling guilty in some way. It shouldn't have turned out like this. I watched as they were killed, one by one, leaning over the low wall, their heads falling onto the earth and turning it red. Somehow I knew that the earth receiving their blood was local to here. I got the feeling that it was Ugijar where this happened.

All I remembered as the sword came down on my neck was that my prayers had not been answered. At that moment of death came the realization that I had lost faith in God because my prayers to Him asking for a safe release from my captors had been ignored.

I had lost my faith in that moment. And I had not forgiven my killers.

When this buried memory from another life was recalled, I came to the immediate realization that the key to my healing lay in forgiving those people who had killed me. So I mentally forgave them, and Marcus instantaneously let out one of his loud shouts.

That memory was so unexpected. I had never considered the possibility that I had lived in this area before. It's difficult to describe remembering a past life. I knew it was me but I was in a different body. I knew that I was male, a fervent believer in God and I was burning with faith.

The more Marcus released my muscles, the clearer the memories became. I got the feeling I had lived in the convent when it was a Franciscan friary. I recalled sweeping objects, sacred artefacts, into a cloth so that I could hide them. I don't know who I was hiding them from, but I was in a great hurry. Unfortunately, at the end of this session my neck was still locked though it felt a bit better.

"We have one more session to go. We're getting there but there's still a part that is being very resistant to release," said Marcus. "Would you be prepared to take a remedy?"

"What sort of remedy?" I asked.

"A flower remedy. I'd like to suggest you take some kissamota."

I'd heard of the Bach flower remedies which can be bought from most health shops, but I'd never heard of kissamota. It was obviously not a Bach remedy.

"Of course. I'll try anything to try and get this neck sorted out."

Marcus gave me three tiny pills and asked me to take one a day for the next three days. My last massage was in three days time so I would have to take the last pill on the day of my last massage.

Once Marcus had finished the massage Nicky joined us. Nicky suddenly said, "There is something hidden in that convent. Scrolls."

We both looked at her. Where did that statement come from?

"Why do you say that?" I asked.

"I don't know. I've just got this really strong feeling that there are scrolls in there."

"Are you a psychic or something?" I asked.

"I used to work in that field. When I lived in England I helped the police with locating lost people and stuff like that."

"So what makes you think there are scrolls?"

"It's not me, Nicky, that thinks that. Those words that came out of my mouth just came through me. Somebody from the other side has used me as a channel to give you that information." The other side? She must mean dead people. Somebody who had died was trying to get a message to me. Was it my cousin John, the cousin who had lent me the money for the convent?

"Please don't mention what you just said to anybody. I know what Ugijar is like for gossip. I don't want that rumor getting round." Marcus and Nicky promised not to say a word.

A few days later I returned to Marcus and Nicky's for my final massage. In the last session I knew that we were going to be going more deeply into my resistant neck. This would be the make or break session. I had taken the kissamota remedies over the previous three days but I had not noticed any particular effect. I set off on the 30 minute drive along the high mountain roads from Valor, 1000 meters above sea level to Picena, passing the entrance to the Ragua pass on the way. The sign was flashing to say it was closed that day. The Ragua pass is the high pass over the Sierra Nevada mountains, over 2000 meters above sea level. The winter snow falls thickly at that height.

It was a particularly beautiful evening with the most unusual cloud formations illuminated by a slowly setting sun, from the most delicate lilac through to the deepest, richest maroon. It was as if heaven was meeting earth, breaking through the ethers to give us mortal souls a glimpse of the beauty of that plane of existence. I had to stop and take a photo. When I got back into the car and started to drive off I was startled by a horrendous crunch in my neck. This was nothing like the crack from a chiropractic or osteopathic adjustment. This was a crunch so devastating that I thought my neck might have broken. I hadn't even been moving my head when the crunch had happened. I pulled in to the side of the road, hardly daring to move. Was I paralyzed? Gingerly I turned my head. It still moved. I could wriggle my toes and fingers still. What the hell was that crunch about?

When I arrived at Marcus's I told him what had happened. He looked pleased.

"Had you taken the remedy?"

"Yes."

"I was hoping something like that would happen. A release. That's a good sign."

"It was pretty scary. I've never had a crunch like that in my neck before."

"Something has shifted. You know how blocked your neck has been. You've had five long sessions and you've still got a lock in your neck. Now I hope we can get to the core of your problem. I'm not doing the body massage today, I'm just doing your neck."

I climbed up onto the couch and lay on my back. The wood burner was burning well today and the room was smoke free and nice and warm. Marcus put on some classical music, I closed my eyes and

Marcus started work on my neck. He stroked the back of my neck with long, firm movements. Then, holding my head in both of his hands, he lifted it from the couch and moved it gently in different directions. I felt a bit wary, my neck still felt vulnerable because of the recent crunch. But we both knew that we were going to get to the bottom of this locked neck today, however long it took. Slowly I relaxed into the session as Marcus's fingers worked their way relentlessly into the left hand side of my neck, near the point where it met the skull. I just kept relaxing. I was ready to release whatever it was in my neck that was causing me pain. My mind was focused clearly on my neck. I consciously relaxed each time Marcus found a painful muscle. The session was long but Marcus was persistent.

And then it came to me. A memory of yet another life right here in Ugijar. I knew I was a warrior but I was also a learned man. I could hear the bells in the tower ringing in a fast repetitive way that I knew was the warning signal. It was the same sound as the bells I had heard at the fiesta in Ugijar, the sound that had caused the hairs on my neck to rise. I knew the bell meant 'they're coming' – whoever 'they' were. My heart was beating furiously in my chest and I knew I was in terrible danger. Clutching a metal casket, which I knew needed to be hidden, I ran for the entrance to the tunnel. I must hide it before they get me. This mustn't fall into the wrong hands, but neither could I destroy it.

Then the scene changed. They wanted me to talk. They wanted me to tell them something but I would not say what they wanted me to say, so I was subjected to the most horrendous tortures. A red hot poker was pushed through my neck from behind, right through to the other side. The cruelty of these people defied belief. How could one human being be so cruel to another? The heat was a searing heat. I could not believe that I was still alive and experiencing such pain. How could I remain conscious through this? Then I must have lost consciousness because the next memory was of my head moving from side to side as my body was being moved. Maybe my neck was broken. I think I was on the back of a cart because I could hear the sound of cart wheels. All I knew was this searing pain in my neck as I drifted in and out of consciousness.

I was to be executed by the sword. But somehow the sword did not come down cleanly on my neck. So there I was with my head hanging off, the smell of my blood in my nostrils, still hanging on to life by a thread, falling in and out of consciousness. I prayed to be released from this, just as I had been praying since the torture had started, but no release had come. At that moment my faith died along with me. A name came to me as I died, my name. It sounded like Sauello.

Marcus let out another of his large shouts. What timing! How did he know what was going on in my mind? "We've got there. Right to the core."

I didn't reply. I couldn't speak.

"There was definitely a beheading in there," he said. "A beheading and maybe torture too."

I couldn't even manage a grunt. How did he know? Could he read my mind?

"You know there was a big battle in the valley just below here, don't you?"

I didn't know that but I still couldn't speak.

"Are you okay?"

I was actually shivering despite the warmth of the room. When I did speak my voice was shaky.

"I need a drink."

I was in shock and I needed sweet tea. Marcus made me a cup of tea sweetened with honey as I shakily sat up. I did not speak until I had drunk my tea. I couldn't. I had just been tortured and beheaded. No wonder those memories were buried so deep. It's not the sort of thing one wants to remember.

"What happened?" Marcus asked. He looked concerned. I suspect

I was as white as a sheet.

"I was beheaded." My voice was a strangled whisper.

"I thought so."

"And tortured."

"Tortured? Maybe you were a Templar then. They were subjected to the most horrific tortures."

"I was in Ugijar."

"I'm not surprised. I think you've been brought back to that convent to clear up a lot of darkness. It may have been a convent but that place is stuffed with history."

"I know. It's ancient. I think it dates back to Roman times."

"What makes you think that?"

"Because I can see the earth walls have been built on stone foundations. You know there was a Roman Temple dedicated to Athena in Ugijar, don't you? I think the convent was built on the foundations of the temple."

This was one of the legends that had been handed down through the generations. There was reputed to have been a Roman temple dedicated to the Goddess Athena and Ulyssees came to visit the temple. That's why the local secondary school is known as 'Instituto Ulyssees'.

So here I was, back again in the Alpujarra mountains, only this time it was in the 21st century and I was yoga teacher and I was a woman.

As I sat on the edge of the massage couch drinking my sweet tea I noticed a picture on the wall that looked familiar. It was a man smiling enigmatically and holding up a pointed finger. It was as if he was looking directly at me. It was Da Vincis painting of John the Baptist. He had been looking down on me as I had re-lived my torture and beheading. What was he pointing at? Where did he fit in to this mystery?

So maybe I had had two lives in the convent. If so, in both those lives I was beheaded and in one I was tortured. It was difficult to gain clarity because of the similarities of the lives. In both lives I was killed, my prayers were not answered and I died without faith. But at least now I knew that the key to my healing was in forgiving those who had killed me, and in forgiving myself, and not holding myself responsible for the deaths of my brothers.

CHAPTER ELEVEN

I felt inspired and excited whenever I learned more about the history of the convent. The information from my neighbors had been a complete surprise. The University of Granada was quite a way from Ugijar so I could not understand how the convent could have been linked to it. The bus took five hours to reach Granada. How long must it have taken to get there on horseback? I needed to speak to the priest to glean some more information. Everybody in town knew the priest. He was young, not bad looking and wore an extremely large metal brace over his teeth. Actually half the population of Ugijar wore metal braces. It seems to have been the speciality of the local dentist. I wanted to see the painting and the book of the church that my neighbor had mentioned.

The church door was open so I went straight in. That was strange. The back of the church was full of gypsies and there was none of the usual congregation. A service was about to start, so I sat down near the edge of one of the rows, somewhere between the gypsies and the altar. Out came the altar boys, decked in robes and carrying candles. The priest entered, also in robes. People stood and the service started. It was all in Spanish and I didn't understand any of it. After a few minutes I gave up trying to follow the service and I just sat. It was a massive church for a relatively small town. It had huge pillars holding up the roof and behind the pillars were various alcoves housing paintings. The ceiling was high and domed. After the service I went in search of the priest. He was in an ante-room with a few of the gypsies. He looked surprised to see me but he obviously knew who I was. Let's face it, everybody knew who I was because this town was a hotbed of gossip.

"Hello. I want to see the book of the church," I stated.

He looked directly at me. He couldn't have been more than 30 years old and he didn't look like priest material. What had led him to commit his life to the church at such a young age?

"The book of the church," he repeated.

"Yes."

"Wait. One minute".

He asked the gypsies to wait and picked up a bunch of keys that were hanging on the wall. "Come!"

I followed him out of the church to an adjoining building where he unlocked the door. I was so excited. The book of the church must be very old and was bound to list the former priests and maybe the Templars too. It might also give me an idea of the date of origin of the convent. I could picture it in my mind, a huge, ancient, leather bound book with a lock on it. The room we entered was simple, bookshelves lining one wall. He reached up and took down a large book and opened it. It didn't look particularly old or impressive and when it was opened I could see names written in lists, not in copper plate ink script like I had imagined but in biro. He handed me a pen.

"You write."

"Write what?" I asked.

"The name of the dead person."

"What dead person?"

"The person you want to have written in the book of the church."

It was clear that there had been a breakdown in communication here. It turned out that today was known as the Day Of the Dead, Dia de Los Muertas, and the mass I had just attended was the mass for the deceased, for the ancestors.

"No, I don't want this book. I want the book about the history of the church. Historia!"

I could see that now he understood.

"Ah, historia, si."

"I want to find out about the history of the convent and I thought that you had a book about the history of the church."

"The convent has nothing to do with the church."

"Really?"

"Really. I'm certain. The convent was Franciscan and the church is Catholic. They are nothing to do with each other. Totally separate."

"But do you have a book about the church?"

"You mean the book written by the local historian!"

He took a slim red pamphlet from a pile of books on the sideboard and handed it to me. I turned it over and on the back cover was an illustration of the painting that the neighbor had told me about. It was a shocking picture of murder and torture, people being burned alive, hung upside down over blazing fires and being massacred. What a strange painting for the church to have. No wonder it was not on public display. It was definitely a painting of Ugijar, I could clearly see the entrance to the convent and the shrine. The arched doorway with double gates was exactly the same in this painting as it was today. It was the gate of my nextdoor neighbor, the one who had told me about the church painting. Right in the center was a large naked man being tortured. He looked familiar. I think it was me in that other life.

Somebody who witnessed these things must have painted this painting to show later generations what had happened in Ugijar. There was no signature on the painting to indicate who the artist might have been but in the corner I noticed an eight-pointed star. I know this is a symbol associated with the Knights Templars. Was this painted by a Templar?

I left the church feeling confused. The old gypsy had been so determined, desperate in fact, to tell me of the tunnel linking the church with my convent, yet now I was being told there was no connection between the two. And why would the painting have the eight-sided star in the corner?

~

November the eleventh was approaching. The 11:11 day. The number that had brought me to Ugijar. I decided I would have to do something special to commemorate it.

I started the day with a meditation, looking for that still quiet place within me. When I opened my eyes half an hour later I laughed when I saw what was on the ceiling. I had a crystal hanging in the window and the sun had caught it in such a way that four straight lines of rainbow light had appeared as 11:11 in huge numerals above me, 11:11 in colored light!

I headed for the convent. At 11 in the morning I would like to bless the fountain. To me this was a most important day and the ideal day to bless the fountain and decide on a name for the center. There was nobody there when I turned up at the convent. There was a lorry parked up the side. Maybe the workers were having their breakfast in a nearby bar. It was the norm here to work from eight until ten and then go for breakfast. I waited an hour and then returned. Still nobody. Miguel had the only key. I couldn't get in so I rang him on his mobile.

"Miguel where are you?"

"I am in my home in Cadiar."

"Are you coming to the convent today?"

"No. Not today."

"What about the other men? Are they working today?"

"No."

"Why not?"

"No today it is not possible."

"Why is it not possible?"

"Not today. How you say? I not knowing the words."

Miguel's English could be very poor when it suited him.

"Where is the key?"

"I have it here at my home."

Home is Cadiar, at least half an hour's drive away.

"Well I can't get into the convent without the key. In future you must leave the key with somebody in Ugijar if you are not going to work."

There was no point in getting angry. I knew that whatever happened I would not be able to get into the convent by 11am. It was already quarter to eleven.

This was when living life by signs could get difficult. Was this a lesson in being organized, grounded and prepared or was this a sign that today was not the day to have a special ceremony? I decided not to let it get me down. I had had expectations of standing in the courtyard wafting incense around but that's the trouble with having expectations. If they don't materialize it can disappoint you.

'Whatever happens, happens right.'

Anthony's words again. He was a wise man, a Daoist, which is one of the ancient wisdoms of China.

I decided to sit on the doorstep and be near the convent at 11:11am on 11th day of the 11th month and I would wait and see what happened at that special moment. So I sat on the step with my eyes closed and waited, silently asking for a sign. What would it be? A pealing of bells or a person I knew turning up?

I sat on the worn stone step, leaning against the heavy old wooden door, keeping my toes tucked under in case they got run over by a passing car. Calle de Los Meridas was a one-way street and not much wider than the width of a car. With my eyes closed and my inner gaze at the point between my eyebrows, I could hear a car approaching. It pulled up and stopped right beside me. I heard the car door open and somebody getting out. I opened my eyes to see who had been brought to my door at this significant moment. It was the local policeman. What did he want? I avoided looking directly at him. That must have looked very suspicious.

"Are you the owner of the convent?" he asked in Spanish.

I looked over in his direction as if I had only just noticed him.

"No Spanish, no hablo espanol," I replied, pretending I didn't understand.

"Do you have a key to get in?"

"No entiendo, I don't understand."

"Where are the builders?"

I didn't know what this was about. Why would the police be coming here? This was the last thing I had expected to happen. I shook my head and shrugged my shoulders, then I stood up and walked off in the direction of the internet café. I didn't fancy getting involved with the police today. Gabriel was inside the internet cafe. I asked him about the book that his family owned. Once more he promised to get it back from his sister.

A few days later the builders appeared again. Miguel's brother arrived but there was no sign of Miguel and no explanation of his absence. Ten days after starting work, they were still clearing rubble in the dumper truck, so much for Miguel's estimate of 'a day or two'. Somebody from the town hall came to see what was going on. I was told that I must appoint an architect because the work had been classed as reconstruction rather than renovation, but I could continue the work whilst the architect drew the plans. The maths teacher at the local secondary school had a second job as an architect and so he was appointed to oversee the work. I helped him with the measuring which took a whole day. There was one room that we could not measure because we could not access it. That was the room that adjoined the tower of the museum, formerly the church tower. The upstairs terrace had completely collapsed, leaving the entrance door to this mystery room totally inaccessible. So he guessed the measurements.

I was presented with the first bill for the building work. It seemed a bit steep but the lawyer checked it over, said it was fine and wrote out the cheque for Miguel on my behalf. The entire front section of the roof had now been completely removed and the first floor of the convent lay naked, exposed to the sky for the first time in hundreds and hundreds of years. Then it started to rain.

I was lying in bed in the apartment when I first heard the sound of water. It was raining. That was the first rain we had had since I had arrived seven weeks ago. Up until now the weather had been bright, sunny and dry, though sometimes cold because of the altitude. It soon became clear that this was not just a shower but torrential rain. I thought of the convent sitting there with no roof, getting soaked and I tried not to worry.

'Worry is a pointless exercise,' I often told my yoga students. Now I was having a chance to put my advice into practice. There was nothing I could do about it.

The rain was relentless. It rained for 24 hours without pause. I rang Miguel to ask him to cover the roof with plastic but he assured me it was not a problem. Another 24 hours passed and still there was no let up in the rain. It was not like English rain that varies in its intensity. This rain had only one setting. Torrential. I rang the architect at the town hall and he came down to take a look. The upstairs floors were deep in water and it had started to seep through and was dripping into the floor below.

"It needs plastic," said the architect. "If water gets into these earth walls they can collapse." That was all I needed to hear. There I was stuck in the apartment on my own listening to the dreadful weather outside. My imagination started to run wild and I had visions of the whole building collapsing. When the wind started up it was too much. I could not sleep. I could not rest. I rang up the builder and insisted it was covered in plastic.

"That's not possible because if we put plastic sheeting up then the rain will simply collect in large pools in the plastic and cause more damage when the plastic gives way causing a torrent of water to gush into your place," I was told.

Once more I felt really alone and had the feeling that I had taken on more than I could handle. Was he telling the truth or was he just too lazy to go out in the wind and rain?

"Just do it," I insisted.

The intensity of the weather was driving me mad. The high winds blew the heavy rain against the windows of the apartment day and night. I couldn't stand it. All I could think of was the effect this would be having on the convent. I tried to concentrate on the book I was reading, *Autobiography of a Yogi* by Paramhansa Yogananda, but the weather was so extreme I was constantly distracted. I picked up the photo of Babaji from my bedside table. Babaji is a yogi who had reached enlightenment so he supposedly had full Divine Consciousness. In which case he would be able to hear me… "Stop the rain now," I begged. "If you do then I will not doubt your existence."

The rain continued unabated. I thought I would go mad if it didn't stop. There was only one thing to do. I got into the car and drove to the shopping center in El Ejido an hour's drive away. Cocooned from the weather in the controlled air conditioning of this recently built indoor shopping mall, this was the only place where I could go and not hear the sound of the wind and rain. I wandered around the shops aimlessly and sat in cafes drinking coffee, waiting for the weather to change.

Life down by the coast in El Ejido and especially in Roquetas was much easier than life up the mountain. More people spoke English, there was a choice of supermarkets and plenty of tourist shops. There were internet cafes, international phone booths where you could phone England for a fraction of the cost of the phone boxes in Ugijar and lovely hotels where one could use the facilities even as a non-resident. Because the terrain down by the coast was level I could walk for miles and miles along the tracks of the large natural park, which nestled between the Mediterranean sea and the plastic greenhouses. In the park I could see the flamingos flying in to land on the salt marshes. An hour away from Ugijar, yet a world away.

Finally, after seven days and seven nights of the relentless drumming of rain on the apartment windows, I woke up to silence.

There was an incredible stillness, as if nature was breathing a sigh of relief. I ventured out into the garden to survey the damage. The water in the swimming pool was completely hidden by the leaves and debris that had blown into the water. Plants were lying flattened on the ground in places where the soil had been washed away. The outdoor table and chairs were lying on the terrace below the level of the apartment, broken where they had been battered against the wall in the violent wind and rain. I dreaded going down to see the convent but I knew I had to. The convent had been a wreck to start with but now it was enough to make me want to cry. The water was still forming puddles on the floor of the living room and it was slowly dripping through the floors and onto the ground below, taking large chunks of the ceiling with it. Five men had been sent in to try and clear up the mess and to make up for lost time. When the bill came it was ridiculously high.

"I want an itemized bill showing who is working each day and how many hours they work." I addressed this demand to Miguel's brother because Miguel was being very difficult to contact.

"No problem," I was told. "I will do that for you today."

When the itemized bill came I could see that everybody was being paid 100 euros a day. That was not our agreement and so I refused to pay. It was 130 euros for the main man, 100 for the assistant and 70 for the laborers. They must have thought I was stupid if they thought I would pay this amount. We had a heated discussion and in the end I agreed to pay part of the bill. Christmas was looming and I was going back to England to visit my family.

"You had better stop work," I told Miguel's brother. "Don't start again until I return from England at the end of December and we can go through those figures again. This was not what we had agreed."

I flew back to the familiarity of England for a two-week break; from a distance I could reflect on things with more clarity. Whatever happened I was committing to this project for a year. This was my dream, to have a yoga center. So often I see how lives can end very suddenly and people die without having fulfilled their dreams. So many people think they will do what they want to do in ten years... or when they retire... or when they have the money... or when they leave home. My cousin John had just embarked on his dream of renovating his Sussex mansion when he died. In fact he was clearing the track of his property on the morning of his death, the first task to be done before the building work started. I did not want to end my life with regrets. I wanted to have a go at fulfilling my dream and even if it didn't work out at least I would die knowing I had tried. So giving up on the convent at this stage was not an option.

CHAPTER TWELVE

So, like it or not, I had to return to Ugijar after Christmas. I needed to sort things out with Miguel so that work on the convent could continue. Arriving back in Spain felt like coming home. I picked up a hire car at the airport and headed up the mountain. At first the roads were wide and not too windy, huge expanses of tarmac expertly cut through the rocks. These brand new roads, built with the help of EU funding, were magnificent. You hardly felt the gradient. We were climbing quite quickly, mountainous terrain whichever way you looked. Here and there I spotted the remains of the old, single-track mountain road that until a couple of years ago was the main route up the mountain. It was not much wider than the width of a car, so I couldn't imagine what would have happened if two vehicles had met on one of the hairpin bends. It would surely have been impossible to reverse. Later I found out that the journey to Ugijar used to take three hours. With the new road it was now not much more than an hour. The new road had only been open for three years so this part of Spain was only just opening up to outsiders.

The new road did not reach quite to Ugijar. At Cherin, eight kilometers from Ugijar, there was a sudden change in road quality. Not only sudden but extreme. I braked sharply as I entered Cherin but I could not miss the potholes as the entire road was potholed. I was forced to slow down. Here the road was narrow and the bends were sharp. But the scenery was fantastic. I meandered through beautifully tended olive groves, one eye on the road and one eye on the scenery. Huge tracts of land were terraced. The scent of orange blossom filled the air. The pink of the almond blossom contrasted with the deep rich red of the earth. There were very few houses around, just the odd small farm. Then I turned the corner and saw Ugijar lying in the valley below. Surrounded by unspoilt hills, with a dramatic backdrop of red cliffs, nestled the town. Driving over the small ancient bridge, the car shook violently because of the deep ridges in the tarmac as well as the numerous potholes. I was glad I was driving a hire car. This couldn't be very good for the suspension. The first building I saw as I entered was a hermitage, the hermitage of San Anton. This solid brick and stone building had a tangible presence and provided a powerful entrance to the town. There was definitely something powerful about Ugijar.

I parked the car and walked down to the convent but there was no sign of activity, though the building equipment was still there. I rang Miguel's mobile but there was no answer. I asked at the bars where he normally drank but nobody had seen him.

"I've not seen him for weeks, not since before Christmas," I was told by Javier, the barman at his favorite bar. I didn't know what to do. He had vanished along with his laborers. I needed to get on with the project as soon as possible. I was fed up with renting an apartment. I wanted to live in my own apartment.

After two week of fruitless searching I decided to make a trip to Orgiva, where Miguel lived. There I bumped into Miguel's brother. I saw him before he saw me, which was fortunate because he looked very ill at ease.

"Where is Miguel?" I demanded. "He seems to have disappeared off the face of the earth."

"I don't know," came the reply, though his brother was unable to look me in the eyes as he spoke.

"What do you mean you 'don't know'? Miguel is supposed to be working on the convent."

"I really don't know. He doesn't answer his mobile and nobody has seen him. He has disappeared. He has not even been to see his mother in Granada hospital, even though she is dying."

It was true. He was nowhere to be found. I tried every possible source to trace him but each time I hit a blank wall. I didn't have a choice. I knew that I was going to have to find a new builder as soon as possible because I could not leave the convent without a roof and open to the elements. The whereabouts of Miguel would have to remain a mystery for now.

~

Posters had suddenly appeared all over town advertising the horse show which was about to arrive. Within days the common land at the entrance to town was transformed into stables and soon the main road was full of lorries and horseboxes, unloading magnificent horses by the dozen. There must have been at least a hundred horses in town and their neighing kept stirring distant memories in me. There was something about the sound of the town full of horses that took me back in time.

For four days there were horse competitions and displays. Handsome Spanish men in their tuxedos and panama hats cantered around town on their beautiful horses. There were riders as young as five, dressed in the same way as their fathers, sitting tall and proud, natural riders even at such a tender age.

The shows were amazing. I was so delighted to be experiencing dancing horses in a setting like this. They trotted slowly, lifting their graceful, slender legs in time with the music. It was magical. The horses were beautifully cared for, healthy and glowing with perfectly groomed manes.

The same couldn't be said for the majority of the local animals. There was everything else in this town except for a vet, which I thought was quite telling. I had seen shocking cruelty. Kittens were tied in plastic bags and thrown in the bushes to die. Or they were drowned at birth. I had seen donkeys with huge gaping sores and cats without eyes. Dogs were often kicked if they got in the way and every cat I had come across ran away as soon as any human appeared. A few dogs and cats had lost their tails. Several times I had seen children walking along the street carrying newly born puppies that were shaking with cold or fear, holding them as if they were toys. When I suggested the puppies needed to be back with their mother I would be offered the animal in return for some euros. Half of the dog population was injured or diseased, I had seen dogs limping along the road covered in mange and weeping sores. Most foreigners ended up giving some of these animals a loving home. Many foreigners had as many as six dogs and cats.

Only one local man seemed to have any compassion for these poor creatures and he was the local photographer. Every day at five o'clock the strays gathered outside his shop and he put food out for them. To see the state of those animals who gathered outside waiting for food was a sorry sight indeed.

Now I had discovered officialdom in Ugijar. Absolutely everything had to be done in triplicate and stamped by the town hall. This made the wheels of progress move very slowly. The town hall in the square was a place for practicing patience because there was usually a long wait to see anybody or to get anything stamped. One day I was walking down past the convent towards the town hall with the usual pile of documents when I was stopped by a complete stranger. She was English.

"Hi," she said. "It's you that has bought that old convent, isn't it? Well listen," she said, urgently, "you might think that I am quite mad, but I have a message for you. You will find what you are looking for."

I had to confess that I was not actually looking for anything at that point.

"I have been having these dreams and you kept popping up in them. When I saw you I instantly recognized you from my dream. I was told that I had to give you this message. I didn't know whether I ought to say anything or not because you might think I was a bit mad, but I know Marcus the masseur and he said that it would be okay to tell you, you would be open minded enough to hear this message for what it is."

I was intrigued. "I will find what I am looking for?"

"Yes. And what you find will enable you to complete the work on the convent."

Now I was really interested. I did not have enough money to do all that needed to be done, perhaps between a third and a half of the work. Nobody knew this as I had not told anyone. My intention was to employ the builders until I ran out of money, knowing that I could not complete the renovations. I had been wondering what was going to happen when the money ran out.

"I'd love to have a look inside the building," she said. "My bedroom window looks directly into the front of the convent."

Karalyn, as she was called, had bought the property directly opposite. Her windows were just two meters from my windows because of the narrowness of the streets. She could indeed look right in to my front rooms.

"I have the key on me," I said. "Come in and have a look now if you like."

Unlocking the door we stepped into the hallway. There was a particularly strong presence inside that hit me like a brick wall. I tried to ignore it. Silently we wandered around. When we walked into the back hall, the room where I had had difficulty breathing when I had first entered it, the room that had not been used or occupied for many years, Karalyn shivered.

"Ooh, I have come out completely in goose pimples!" she exclaimed.

At least she can breathe, I thought to myself. We stood in silence once more and as we stood there I begin to feel a swirling of energy around me. I was not imagining this. It was far too powerful and clear to be my imagination. I was instantly transported back in time. I heard horses and lots of activity. I was in a mad panic and I was calling out instructions to somebody. The whole atmosphere was one of fear, death and panic. There was the stench of fresh blood in the air, hot and pungent. I could hear screaming and a bell ringing loudly and repeatedly, the same speed and rhythm as the bell during the fiesta, which had caused the hairs on the back of my neck to stand on end. The horses were neighing, obviously terrified. The layout of the hall was different then, with a huge, open door leading out onto a track, and trees outside. It was a garden or an orchard and several horses were tethered to the trees. There were balustrades around a stairwell that led down to a cellar or a tunnel. This was very near the doorway. I was going down to hide something but I knew I would have to be really quick. We had to delay them at all costs. I was carrying a metal chest. There were sacred scrolls inside. These had been put in my care and I was to guard them with my life.

"Lock the door after me!" I screamed and down the stairs I went with a pounding heart, down into a tunnel.

A sigh from Karalyn brought me sharply back to the present.

"Did you feel that?" she asked.

"What?"

"That strange energy. I just had a strange flashback. I hung myself from the rafters in here once."

"When?" I asked.

"It was as if I was transported back in time. I had rushed out of the church into here and I had some keys in my hand. There was a door on the other side of the courtyard. I ran across the courtyard knowing I had to hide the keys somewhere where they couldn't be found. I locked the church door and the one in this room. I threw the keys into a cellar or a tunnel then I locked the tunnel door with the small key. I put this key in my mouth and tried to swallow it – which was difficult because it was so big, not as big as the one you have got, but still big, and then I hung myself from the wooden beam in the ceiling. I could hear people banging on the doors trying to get in. I must have been a monk because I was wearing these rough robes."

I told Karalyn of my experience, mentioning the chest but not the fact that it contained scrolls, and we looked at each other in astonishment.

"So you and I must have been here together in that life." I looked across at Karalyn.

"Yes." she replied.

"I went down some steps to hide something."

"I know. I was buying you time. I locked the door after you."

"The stairs must have been around here somewhere," I said.

I silently located the place on the floor where the steps would have been. I noticed a large white feather lying on the exact spot. I scoured the floor for more feathers but this was the only one. A white feather – this was a sign. I often see a white feather at significant moments.

"I wonder if what I hid is still here?"

She wandered around the ground floor and came back to where I was standing, rooted to the spot since that horrible vision of the past.

"Here. They're here".

She was standing on the white feather. The ground floor area of the convent was 450 square meters but she had found the same spot.

"Scrolls. There are scrolls buried here." She pointed down to the floor where the white feather lay. She didn't appear to have noticed it. Or if she had she didn't mention it.

We were both a bit shaken up by this experience. How strange that the first time we found ourselves within the walls of the convent together, the power was so great that the past broke through and was revealed to us. Scrolls? She had used the very same word as Nicky. Not documents, or books, or treasure, or bones. Scrolls.

I wondered whether Marcus or his partner had said something to her.

"Did Marcus mention scrolls to you?" I asked.

"No. Why?"

"Oh, it's just that they mentioned something to me about scrolls."

"They thought that there were scrolls hidden there too?"

"Yes. But listen, please keep this secret. Please don't mention it to anyone. You know what this town is like with the gossip and everything. I don't want rumors of scrolls to start circulating."

"No. I won't tell a soul. Promise."

If there were some scrolls hidden then maybe I ought to search for them. That would mean digging up the floor, not an easy task. I didn't want the scrolls to become common knowledge. For now this secret belonged to Karalyn, Marcus, Nicky and me. But if I was going to attempt to dig them up, then some others would have to be let in on the secret. Karalyn and I discussed the situation. Who could we trust? In the end we decided that Karalyn's partner could be told. He was a building labourer and was strong and muscular, physically perfect for some heavy digging. Then there was Mark the masseur. He was trustworthy. And he was the person who had released the first past life memories for me. He was lean and muscular and strong. Nicky was also a special soul. She could be trusted. She was the person who had given me a message from 'the other side'. Her message was that the scrolls were important writings hidden in the convent and that they must not fall into the wrong hands. In particular they must not fall into the hands of the Catholic church.

"Get them to this person," she had said, writing a name and a phone number on a piece of paper. I had recognized the name as the author of a best selling book on the Holy Grail.

We decided then and there that there was no time to be wasted. The builders were not around at the moment to see what was going on so now would be the ideal time. We contacted everybody we had listed and they all agreed to help. Arrangements were made for the coming weekend. Marcus would bring some spades, Karalyn would bring torches and I would bring the key. We arranged to meet at ten o'clock on Sunday morning outside the convent. Nobody else was being told of our intentions. I was starting to get excited. I felt as if I was in a real life adventure story.

Sunday came and I got up early. It was cold and I put several layers of clothes on. Then my mobile phone rang. It was Marcus. "Look outside," he said.

I opened the wooden shutters and gasped in disbelief. The garden was thick with snow. Marcus and Nicky further up the mountain were completely snowed in for three days. I took this as a strong sign from the universe that now was not the time to unearth the scrolls! Snow like this was virtually unheard of in this region. High in the Sierra Nevada mountains above us the snow would lie all winter, but not down in the Alpujarras. This year there was snow all the way down to the coast. Andalucia had never seen anything like it. Temperatures in the valley dropped to minus 20 degrees. It was so cold in the apartment that I could not breathe the air. The only thing I could do was to stay in bed with a hot water bottle and keep a sheet over my head and breathe through the cloth of the sheet. The central heating and the hot water had packed up completely and the wood for the fire was too damp to burn. The apartment was the former garage of the villa and had obviously been built without insulation. I hoped I wouldn't die of hypothermia. I could not get down to the coast because of the state of the roads. Helicopters were brought in after a few days to airlift stranded people in their farmhouses. These fincas are approached by tracks which, because of the terrain, are never level. Seventeen people died of the cold in the village along the valley. Many of the houses in these mountains were not heated save for an open fire. If the firewood gets damp or runs out then people die from the cold. For the first time in living memory Ugijar was actually cut off. And the dig for the scrolls was postponed. That convent was not going to give up its secrets easily.

The severe weather lasted about two weeks and left its mark on the landscape. The garden was in a terrible state. The oranges and lemons had been frozen on the tree. They were rock solid, transparent with ice. All the fruit trees had died. Some of them were over 50 years old. There were dead bodies of cicadas and a small bird floating in the swimming pool. Unfortunately, the rat which lived in the garden had survived, because I could see fresh droppings on the terrace. After the silence of the snow, the countryside was now alive with the sound of axe against wood as people started to replenish their dwindling stocks of logs. At least there was plenty of firewood available now because of all the dead trees. I watched as lorries of freshly cut logs wound their way up the mountain. The high peaks of the Sierra Nevada were heavily laden with pristine white snow, the sun was out and the birds were singing again.

The bad weather had affected Marcus and Nicky who had made the decision to leave the Alpujarras. They had decided that life in the mountains was too difficult, so they packed up their camper van, added a few stray dogs and took the ferry to Majorca. Karalyn's relationship had not survived the intensity of being snowed in together and they had split up. So the digging party was now scattered. How was I going to dig now?

Work on the convent was at an absolute standstill. The best builder in town was not available for at least a year. I couldn't possibly wait that long. The only few people available were the builders that nobody wanted because their work was poor. I asked everybody I knew for help and it was Karalyn who came up with a suggestion.

"Why don't you ask Tom? My ex used to work for him and he's a great builder. He'll do you a good job."

"But when is he available?"

"I don't know. You'll have to talk to him. Do you want me to give him a ring now? I've got his number on my mobile."

The following day I met Tom. He had a no-nonsense, down to earth approach. When I told him how much money I could afford he gave me a fixed price for the job. I would have enough money to create an apartment and a yoga studio. The rest would have to wait. That didn't matter. It would mean I would have somewhere to live and somewhere to teach. That was all I needed. What was even better was that Tom was English so I wouldn't have the added problem of communication difficulties, having to speak through an interpreter.

"There's only one problem," Tom told me. "I won't be able to do anything for about six months." Six months! I would have to wait six months? But I didn't really have a choice. Decent builders were like gold dust around here and the fact that I had to wait showed that he was in demand so he must have been good. What could I do but accept? Accept that I would have to wait. Another test of my patience. I had heard it said that the only way to become a patient person was to practice being patient. Here was a wonderful opportunity for me.

Although there would nothing happening on the convent for a while, I could use this time to improve my Spanish and get to know the area a bit better. I started with a visit to the museum which adjoined the convent. It was only open on a Saturday morning. When I arrived I was the only person in there except for the very elderly curator who was in attendance. He was sitting on a chair by the door half asleep.

"Hello. Are you open?"

He jumped at the sound of my voice and slowly pulled himself onto his feet. I don't think the museum got very many visitors.

"Come in, come in. Come and see the museum."

I followed him through the intricately carved door which led into a small entrance hall, dark and dingy.

"Here." He threw open the door on the right and I walked through to find myself standing in a massive church, with high ceilings. I had no idea it would be this big. I had thought that the Catholic church was big but this one was more impressive. I walked towards the front of the church, which was built in the form of a cross, more like a Tau cross rather than a Greek cross. Above me was a massive dome. The original dome had been replaced with a Perspex dome, which was completely out of keeping with the character of this historic building. I could see the sky. This was the advantage of the Perspex; the amount of light which flooded in to the church. Here and there were remnants of ancient wall paintings.

"It's a very special place," the curator told me above the sound of the music. He had classical music playing loudly. "Come upstairs and I will show you the books."

I followed him up a narrow winding staircase which led onto an open balcony looking down onto the church.

"Here!" We climbed more stairs, steeper and narrower than the first and entered a small room crammed with ancient books. I picked one up from the shelf. I didn't even recognize it as Spanish. I would have loved to be able to read them.

"Come!" There was more to see. Up a couple of steps was a tiny room full of rosaries. Nothing but rosaries. Something didn't add up here. I had thought this place was Franciscan, not Catholic. These must have been from a later period, when the Franciscan Friary was in the hands of Catholic nuns. That could be as late as the turn of the century.

This old church was nothing like my convent. I didn't get that feeling of being watched in here. It felt much more alive. I was led through another door into a small kitchen.

"Here the nuns made meals for any passing traveler. They gave travelers a bed and food when they passed through town."

I was not sure what period he was talking about. I did not understand everything he said. In Andalucia the people speak in a particularly strong dialect, often leaving out certain sounds and not completing words.

"The church was lived in by local families until 20 years ago. The owner of the church had put a new floor right across the center to make it into a two-storied house. But one of the wealthy families in

Ugijar have paid to restore the church to its former glory. They took out the floor, collected together all the memorabilia and have created this museum as a gift to the town."

It was nice to hear of an altruistic act like that. I must admit I had found it disconcerting that the oldest religious buildings of the town were allowed to be privately owned. I include my convent in that statement.

"The front door is beautiful," I noted.

"Ah yes, but that door is from another part of Spain. It is not the original one."

That figured. Most of the old church doors I had seen in the local area had been simple, heavy studded wood, except for the door in the convent with the double headed eagle. I had learned a bit more about the convent from my visit to the museum and now at least I knew what was on the other side of the convent wall.

As I left and walked back up Calle de Los Meridas I noticed a modest house with an ancient, dark wood carved door. Looking more closely I could see what had been carved there. A double headed eagle, just like the one in the convent. I knocked on the door and an elderly woman answered.

"Hello, I have just been looking at your door. I wondered if you knew anything about it."

"This is a very old door that has been in my family for many hundreds of years," replied the old woman.

"How many hundred?" I was hoping she could give me an exact date. But all she did was wave her hand over her shoulder to indicate times past.

"Oh many hundreds of years. The answer is lost in the passing of time. Too old, too old, just like me. Too old."

It was frustrating. I felt as though I was scratching at the surface of something very deep but I was unable to find the information I wanted. This door must have come from the Templar church because it was so similar to mine. Gabriel was the man with the answers because his family had the book of the convent but despite my constant requests the elusive book still had not surfaced.

CHAPTER THIRTEEN

It would be at least July before Tom could do anything, meaning that the convent would simply sit there open to the elements for a few more months. How frustrating. I did not understand why there should be all these delays. Was it to test my resolve or was it a sign that there was a block on the project? I had no idea. Living a life according to the signs can be difficult at times like this.

My next door neighbor was not talking to me and when I passed her in the street she spat hatred at me, muttering something unintelligible under her breath. She scooped up dog faeces and either threw them over her garden wall onto my patio or shoved them through the gap in the huge front doors. My patio was littered with her household refuse. She was obviously angry or mentally disturbed. Or both. I asked Rico Santos to find out the problem on my behalf; it turned out that she didn't like the dust that the building work had created. So that was her way of expressing her feelings!

My other neighbor, a youngish woman who yelled and screeched at her children all day, owned the shop next door to the convent. She told me I owed her 600 euros for water and electricity. Because the convent had no water or electricity connected, she had kindly offered to let the builders use her supply. Now I realized that this was not the neighborly help I had thought it was, but was a calculated ruse to get some money out of me.

"How can it possibly be that much?" I asked.

"Your builders have used gallons of water. My bill is really high."

"Show me the bill and I will pay."

Needless to say she would not produce either her electricity bill or her water bill because even if the builders had used water and electricity all day the cost could not have exceeded a hundred euros. This town was ruled by money. Money and religion. And drugs and alcohol. It was not the idyllic small town life that it had appeared to be at first sight. When the shops closed, cocaine was produced and laid on the counter of certain bars to be snorted. Heroin was procured from the port in Almeria and smoked or injected. Cannabis grew fast in this climate, often in local gardens. This town was a haven for alcoholics, being available 24 hours a day and this tended to draw a lot of people with issues around alcohol.

I was wandering down the road past the convent when I saw Karalyn sitting on her doorstep opposite the convent. She spent most of her time sitting there watching the world go by. Her shop sold fair trade clothes, but as she was a 'foreigner' very few local people entered. A woman was sitting next to her. She introduced herself.

"Hello, I'm Sue. You don't know me but Karalyn told me that you are the woman that has bought the convent. I live up in Mairena and run psychic development workshops. I teach dowsing and I wondered if you would give me permission to dowse the convent."

Funnily enough, I had heard of Sue. She was known as Psychic Sue and had worked closely with the police in England as a psychic before moving over to Spain to run her courses. What was it about this area that attracted so many psychics? It seemed to me that suddenly I was surrounded by psychic people! I was happy to give her permission but on condition that I went in with her whilst she was dowsing.

The dowsing took place a few days later. The two of us entered the convent in the middle of the day and yet again I got this eerie feeling of being watched. Psychic Sue took out her dowsing rods and silently walked around the building watching the rods as they parted and crossed. I had not said a word to her about the incident with Karalyn and Karalyn had promised me that she had not mentioned it.

"I want to see if she comes up with the same findings as me. Let's just wait and see what she comes up with," Karalyn said before we went in.

I didn't have to wait long.

"This building is much older than anyone thinks," she began. "There are things hidden here. Documents. Writings. There are scrolls."

She was standing very near to the spot where Karalyn had got goosepimples.

"They are near here somewhere."

She closed her eyes and paused. "There is a small child here. A little girl."

I momentarily wondered if that is who had been watching me. But just as quickly I discarded the idea, for whatever had been watching me had a menacing air about it. No way could it have been a young child.

"Not just a child. There are others."

Who has been watching me?

"There are other things hidden here. Not just scrolls."

I already knew this because I had the memory of taking the sacred objects from the altar in one of my past lives, wrapping them in a cloth and hiding them.

"And there is lots of stuff going on here," continued Sue. "The atmosphere is thick with psychic activity. This place is so very, very old and so much stuff has gone on here. Lots of traumatic stuff. It's a heavy energy."

"I think you're right, Sue. I buried something here in another life. I think it was a metal box of scrolls. After I hid them in the wall I put the earth back so it looked as if it was just a wall and then I sealed them in there with a spell. I drew a symbol in the air just in front of the place where the box was hidden. Like this."

I took a piece of wood that was lying on the ground and drew the symbol in the loose earth on the floor. These memories were coming back to me as I spoke. I didn't even know such things as 'sealing spells' existed. How come I was suddenly remembering all this? Was it because I was there with Sue? I remembered thinking that if anybody came along and tried to dig up the scrolls then that seal would be powerful enough to stop them. I had put it there with the intention of going back later and retrieving the documents myself. It was only meant to be temporary. I had obviously not expected to be killed. I did not realize my return would be delayed by hundreds of years.

I met Karalyn in the bar soon after Sue had left and I told her what Sue had said.

"What did I tell you!" she shouted excitedly. "The exact same words that I used. Scrolls. And where did she think they were?"

"In the same place that you thought!" I replied.

Sue had told me that she was running a psychic development course the following week and asked if she could bring her students along to teach them dowsing. She also agreed that Karalyn and I could come along too. I had never dowsed and welcomed the opportunity to have a go.

A week later we were once again in the convent. This time there were five of us. Myself, Karalyn, Sue, her student called Helen and an American woman, a yoga teacher like me. I was using a crystal pendulum hanging from a chain to dowse. I walked around holding this crystal out in front of me. For a while nothing happened and then when I walked over by the window it was as if the crystal hit an invisible force field. This was the place where the door used to be according to my vision.

"Have you found something?" asked Sue.

"I think there might be something here," I said.

Sue bent down and picked up a white feather in the place I was pointing to. I had not seen the white feather.

"That is a good sign," she said, handing me the feather. Where did this come from? It wasn't the same one as before because I had taken that one home with me. She also picked up a small spiral seashell and handed it to me. "What was that!" exclaimed Karalyn. "I thought I saw a little girl."

Only Sue and I knew about the little girl. I was keeping as much to myself as possible because I was finding all this a bit unnerving, so I thought that if any of this stuff was true, I would rather have the same information coming from as many sources as possible.

"There is a little girl here," confirmed Sue. "She really needs to be moved on. There's a nun too. Perhaps one day soon we can have a clearing ceremony. I have done quite a lot of work in the past clearing earth bound spirits. Or ghosts, which is what most people call them."

I thought I would really like her to get rid of whatever was watching me.

"Now, I would like you to do some automatic writing," she told her students and handed out paper and pens. "All you have to do is walk around and see what impressions you pick up. Anything that comes to your mind write down, however bizarre or irrelevant you might think it is."

Her students wandered around silently, now and then writing notes down in their notebooks. So did Karalyn and I. After about half an hour we gathered in a group in the back hall and compared notes.

It was the turn of the American student first. She read from her notes.

"A lot of sadness. A feeling of loss. I actually found it quite hard to breathe when I was in the back room." That was the room that I had found it hard to breathe in. I had put it down to the dust but maybe it wasn't just that. Maybe it was because of what had happened in there in the past.

"It's a very secretive place. There's definitely something hidden here. They hid something here," she continued. "Scrolls".

The word hung in the air for what seems like ages but was probably only a few seconds. That same word again.

"Death. Abortions. Illegal surgeries." She looked at us in turn. I personally thought that she was way off the mark. Abortions? In here? No way!

"Thanks," said Sue. "Helen?"

"I get a lot of sadness from the place," she started. "Right here in this hall I get the feeling that there has been a suicide. I think someone hung themselves from a rafter."

Karalyn and I met each other's gaze in unspoken communication. We did not say a word but our eyes said it all.

"I get the feeling that there has been sickness here, people dying. There are children here too." She had written a lot of notes in her neat handwriting. All her points had been bulleted in a very ordered manner.

- Wait for the right time
- Very sacred place
- Lots of people lived here over time
- Old ones were left here to die
- It's older than you think
- Look for the history
- One day it will be yours
- Last of the old ones lived here
- They were not all good
- Tell Hilary to wait just a bit longer
- Her time will come and it will be brighter than she envisions
- She has the courage
- It's all in the past

She had not mentioned anything buried, but I reminded myself that she was a student of Sue's, not a fully fledged psychic. So far Marcus's partner Nicky, Karalyn, Sue and the American student had all mentioned hidden scrolls. I had to take note. I was getting the same messages repeated many times. Where are these messages coming from?

~

My belief is that earth is like a school. When we die we leave our physical body behind like an old garment and our individual consciousness enters our astral body. The astral body is an exact counterpart of the physical body but in the astral body we are unfettered. We do not have pain or illness and we only have to intend a change and that change happens. Say for example that on earth we have one leg slightly shorter than the other and so we walk with a limp. Once you die and leave the physical body you will probably say to yourself, 'Right, now I am going to have legs of the same length so I can walk and run easily.' Instantly it is so. If you have a body stiff with arthritis you will leave behind all the stiffness and pain. You can change your appearance at will, though in practice most people keep themselves recognizable as the person they were in their previous incarnation. After death we review the life we have just had and look at what has happened and how we have changed. If we take the school analogy, this is end of year exams. We have set the exam and we are the ones that mark it. There would be no point in cheating as we would be cheating ourselves. There is no God judging us. My belief is that we are each individual consciousnesses and our ultimate goal is enlightenment. Enlightenment is when we become fully realised, when our consciousness is taken to the highest level and we become conscious light. At this level we no longer have an individual ego, though we still have an individual consciousness.

To reach this state it is necessary to give up the ego. It takes a lot of faith to do this and I believe this can be done by following signs when they appear. The signs appear as coincidences or as certain numbers, especially 11 11. For example, if the phone rings at exactly 11 11 then I would take particular note of that phone call. When I was selling my home in Dorset, England I couldn't decide whether to sell it as it was to a private buyer or to sell it to a developer who wanted to knock it down and build flats on the site. One morning the phone rang at 11 11am. Immediately I thought 'who is this ringing me at 11 11?' It was the developer. I took this as a sign and, putting my own thoughts and desires to one side I immediately chose to allow my much loved house to be knocked down. This decision was confirmed as the correct decision to make when I learned that the developers phone number ended in 111! Learning to follow signs is not that easy. Sometimes signs are clear and I know exactly what is expected of me. Other times I have to try and decipher what the signs are trying to say. When the going gets really tough I have to ask myself whether the signs are telling me to give up and go in a different direction or whether it is simply that my faith is being questioned. That to me is the Art of Living.

"What about you Hilary. Did you pick anything up?"

Sue's voice jolted me into the moment.

"Oh, just a feeling of being watched," I said.

A feeling of being watched, an anger, an underlying sinister energy, a darkness, stagnation, claustrophobia and evil. Psychic Sue was right. This place needed clearing.

CHAPTER FOURTEEN

Daily life was pleasant and slow. Nobody rushed around and the general ambiance of the town was pretty laid back. Living in a town this size I saw the same people day in and day out. Which had advantages and disadvantages in equal measure. The advantage was that you could find anybody you were looking for but the disadvantage was that you couldn't avoid anybody if you wanted to. One morning I bumped into Maria, the lawyer.

"Where is Miguel? Have you seen him? He owes me money."

"No Maria. I don't know where he is."

That was true. I didn't have a clue where he had gone. He had left all his tools in the convent but nobody had seen him for months.

We were standing outside the Catholic church with its Islamic doorway. The bells chimed eleven and we waited until they were silent before continuing our conversation.

"They're loud!" I exclaimed.

"Yes," said Maria looking up at the church. "It used to be a mosque, you know, when Ugijar was occupied by the Moors. Behind here, where the medical center is now, was the Moorish graveyard."

"I haven't seen a graveyard up there."

"No. They built the medical center on top of it a few years ago."

What stunning insensitivity. Maybe there was still a residue of Christian/Muslim hatred here. Yet I knew that for many hundreds of years these people lived up here in these mountains in perfect harmony. The Moors had brought so much to this area. Not only the fascinating irrigation system without which this area would be arid, but also the knowledge of silk production and a rich cultural heritage. The scattered villages which clung precariously to the sides of the hills looked exactly like the Berber villages of north Africa.

Sitting in the bar in Ugijar drinking 'mosto', fresh grape juice, I found myself sitting next to a lively Spanish woman. I had not seen her before and I didn't think she was local. It was quite unusual for women to be in a bar alone around here. She turned to me and spoke in English. "Do you live here or are you on holiday?" she asked.

"I'm living here for a year while my property is being renovated, though nothing is happening on it at the moment. I'm waiting for my builder to start."

She did not immediately realize that I had bought the convent, which confirmed to me that she was not a local. It turned out that she was Spanish but she lived in London and came to the Alpujarras as often as she could to stay on her friend's finca (a small farm).

"Do you want to come and see the farm?" she asked.

"Yes, that would be nice. Maybe I could come over one day next week."

"I won't be here next week. I'll be back in London. Why not come up now," she offered.

I was a total stranger, yet she was inviting me to her friend's finca. I soon realized she had ulterior motives. Although she was a woman in her fifties traveling alone, the only way she could get to and from Ugijar was by hitch-hiking. With the lack of traffic around here that was not an easy option. So I drove her back, firstly along the Murtas road and then down a steep, gravely road, deep in the valley. We turned off the gravel track along a rough, earth pathway, the car hitting large boulders and deep potholes.

"I don't think this is suitable for the car. Perhaps I'll pull in here and we can walk," I suggested.

"No, it's fine. It's too far to walk. Another five kilometers or so. Just keep going. It'll be all right." So I kept going, winding up and down, passing the occasional drive that obviously led to other fincas. Then the track suddenly ended. "This is it!"

We got out of the car and I looked around. Directly in front of me was a small, whitewashed building with a couple of out buildings.

There were no other fincas in view, just miles and miles of wild, rugged countryside. The house sat on the side of the hill, in a sheltered position in this hidden valley. There was a stream nearby and a large water tank called a bolsa full of stored water. The house was built in the traditional style with earth walls and wood and cane ceilings. The roof was flat and somebody was lying on a hand-woven carpet, sunbathing. She came down to greet us and I was introduced.

"Do you live here?" I asked.

"I live there," she replied, pointing to what I thought was the chicken house. "With my boyfriend."

She was German, an attractive, educated physiotherapist. Her boyfriend was one of the local gypsies. I recognized him as the brother of the gypsy who played flamenco guitar in a bar in Ugijar.

"Are you coming to the party?"

"You're having a party?"

"Not a big one. Javier's family is coming down to the field for lunch." Javier was the boyfriend.

And so I found myself invited for lunch. Together we prepared a salad with local ingredients. Juicy, sun-ripened, seriously mis-shapen tomatoes from the garden, ugly but sweet and full of flavor, crispy freshly picked organic lettuce, bursting with insect life, olives from one of their trees, a large sweet onion, and hard-boiled eggs from one of their chickens... all piled high in a cobalt blue bowl, hand thrown and decorated by a local potter. A drizzle of olive oil from last year's olive harvest and the juice from a freshly squeezed lemon was the final touch. It looked delicious.

We could hear voices. The first of the guests had arrived, walking down towards the field below the house. I watched as an old door was dragged over to the center of the field to act as a table and everybody lay their contribution to the picnic on the door. Cans of lager, roast chickens from the market in Ugijar, fresh bread from the bakers, bottles of water, fruit, crisps and a bottle of olive oil. The guests ranged in age from 2 to 82 and they were all relatives of Javier. The smallest child was moved around by his upper arm despite his loud protests, his little legs barely scraping the ground as he tried to escape the iron clutch of his mother. He was yanked here and there by his buxom, dark haired mum who couldn't have been more than fifteen. At the end of the meal his face was washed with spit by one of the other gypsies. She spat several times on her hand and smeared it all around the toddler's mouth, drying it on the grubby T-shirt he was wearing.

A boy of about nine came and sat next to me to tell me about his pets. "I have a horse, two snakes, a parrot and three dogs. And three birds in a cage. "

"Do you?"

"Yes. Oh and a monkey."

I didn't believe him but later I found out that this was true. His father worked on the traveling fairground and brought him back an unusual pet after each trip.

When everyone had finished eating and the pile of lager cans was much smaller, the food was cleared away and the door was moved to one side. Then a young gypsy man in his mid-twenties started to sing. Despite his apparent youth, from his mouth came the most beautiful sound, a haunting flamenco melody which reverberated across the valley. Even though I couldn't follow the meaning of the words, I was moved by the passion in his voice. The other men started to clap their hands in a flamenco rhythm and the women stood up and started to dance. Old and young, fat or slim, they hitched up their tops to reveal their midriffs and they swayed to the melody, egged on by some of the men. Girls as young as five or six danced with a grace and expertise that defied their age. Tiny boys stamped their feet, clapping their tiny hands loudly above their heads. I watched in wonder, aware that what I was witnessing was a rare sight – true, authentic flamenco.

Eventually the music trailed off and I found myself deep in conversation with a dark, curly haired gypsy of about forty. He told me that his dream was to open a center for teaching martial arts.

"Why? Do you teach karate or something?" I asked.

"Yes, and Tae Kwondo. I've been doing it for years, since I was a child. I was taught by my father. I used to train for 12 hours a day. Look."

He took a photograph from his wallet, a photo of himself when he was much younger, without his shirt on. His body was amazing; strong firm and muscular.

"This is what my body used to look like when I had time to train, but now I have children, a family to support, so I need to work to support them. My arms are still strong though."

He pulled up his shirt sleeve and showed me his forearm. There were muscles on his muscles. The definition on his arms was like nothing I had ever seen before.

"I used to walk into the mountains and stay there for weeks, building my *chi*. I wanted to learn to levitate so I would do all the oriental exercises to build my energy. I'd do breath control and movements to change the composition of my blood. I wanted to go beyond the physical. I wanted to free my spirit from the physical body. I believe we are spirits in a human body and I want to be free."

I could hardly believe what I was hearing. He had the same dream as me, to be free of the wheel of rebirth, to not keep being reborn on planet earth. *Chi* is pure energy which the Chinese believe permeates everything that exists. In yoga the word for *chi* is *prana*. The nearest English translation is Divine Energy. It is through control of *chi* / *prana* / Divine energy that we can realize this dream. I felt truly humbled meeting this man.

~

The full moon was approaching and we decided that the clearing of the convent should take place on the night of the full moon. Just before midnight five of us gathered together in Karalyn's house directly opposite the convent. Karalyn's house was quite large. On the first floor were two separate apartments and on the ground floor was the shop behind which was a large covered courtyard. Below was a cellar. We formed a circle in the courtyard. Psychic Sue, the American student, Karalyn, me and Helen. Sue lit some herbs and incense and protected each of us in turn with the incense and with prayer. She did this by filling the area around our physical body with incense smoke. She called it 'smudging'. Karalyn's little Yorkshire terrier Boo sat watching us, staying close to her side. Then, clutching candles and torches we crossed the road and gathered in the rear hall of the convent. Boo followed, close on Karalyn's heels. "He'd better stay behind," suggested Psychic Sue. So Karalyn took him upstairs and locked him in the flat.

In the convent we formed a circle in the back room where I had found the white feather and the seashell. Sue placed a lighted candle in the center of the circle. Then it began.

Sue invited any souls who wished to be moved on and into the light to enter the circle. It was very dark in the hall and we were all together as a group of females but I felt no fear. We stood there holding hands and waited. Then we all became aware of activity. A light appeared upstairs. Karalyn felt a small child clinging onto her leg. I became aware of lots of souls coming through my body towards the center of the circle. I had never felt anyone go through me before but as it was happening I knew exactly what it was. As they entered the circle we silently blessed them and guided them towards the light. There were dozens of souls. It was so strange how we could just sense their presence. At one point, we all became aware of a soul standing near the door, reluctant or afraid to enter. We had this awareness without speaking to each other. On and on it went, more and more souls entering the circle; I was stunned by the sheer number of them.

Finally, I don't know how much later, the activity stopped and after a final prayer we unlinked our hands and were smudged with incense once more.

"Phew, there were loads," gasped Karalyn.

"At least three dozen," agreed Sue.

We left the convent, locking the door behind us and went our separate ways. Hopefully that should change the energy of the convent.

The next morning I got a phone call from Karalyn. Despite the protection, the smudging and the prayers, something had happened.

"Hilary. Are you okay?" she asked.

"Yes I'm fine. Why?"

"Nothing happened when you got home?"

"No. Everything's fine. What about you, are you okay?"

"Not really. When I got back from the convent yesterday I opened the main door and Boo was standing there whimpering and shivering. He leaped straight into my arms. He was terrified."

"How could he have got downstairs? You locked the apartment door."

"Exactly. I went upstairs and the door was wide open. Nobody else has a key to that place so I couldn't understand why the door was open. How could it have opened?"

"What did you do?"

I would have turned round and walked out, but Karalyn was made of stronger stuff.

"I went in and couldn't believe what I saw. Every single door and window in the place was open. All the kitchen cupboards, the wardrobe. Everything. Even the French doors were open. Nobody has ever been able to open those old doors. They were jammed solid with age. And there they were, wide open."

"Oh my god. What did you do?"

"I went downstairs to the shop to check out the shop and the large clothes rack had been moved right to the center of the shop. Nothing else was touched. Just the clothes rack. Boo was going crazy. He was so scared he was shaking like a leaf."

Karalyn went to bed as usual, that night, which I think was very brave of her. As she lay there she clearly heard the sound of chanting coming from the cellar, as there were a group of monks chanting. I had thought it a bit odd that she had a cellar yet the convent didn't. After all, her cellar was less than three meters from my front door.

"Call Sue and let her know."

Psychic Sue came straight down to Ugijar to investigate.

"There is a negative vortex of energy. In all my years of doing psychic work I have only once come across a vortex before. I want you to close the living room door and not use that room until I have had a chance to clear it."

The following day I went round to visit Karalyn and we sat in her bedroom talking about the events that had transpired. Her bedroom was opposite the convent and her living room was almost opposite the screeching neighbor's shop. Both rooms had a balcony. As I wandered onto the balcony I could see activity happening on the tiled area outside the shop.

"Hey, come and look at this Karalyn. What's going on out here?"

Huge drapes had been hung in front of the shop window and red carpets had been laid on the road. Flowers and plants had been placed all around. Flower petals had been laid around the edges of the carpet in beautiful mandala designs. A table had been put on the step with a kneeling cushion in front of it. Standing on the white cloth on the table was a plate of bread and a jug of wine. It was an altar.

An altar directly opposite the vortex. This was unreal.

"What the hell...!"

Karalyn was a bit spooked. She had taken everything in her stride up until now but this was really getting to her.

"I don't like it. I don't understand it."

"But how can you be frightened?" I asked. "Don't you see that the vortex is going to be cleared by this?"

"Who is going to clear it?" she asked.

"The priest from the Catholic church. He doesn't know that he is going to be clearing it but he is," I laughed.

We did not have to wait long. Looking to the right we saw a procession approaching. The smell of the incense and the sound of the band preceded the appearance of the altar boys carrying candles. The priest was being followed by the entire church congregation. He stopped directly opposite and looked straight up at us. His eyes meet our eyes in turn. He knelt at the altar and began to pray. He called out a prayer and the congregation responded with the refrain. He broke the bread and sipped the wine. The petals blew gently in the soft breeze. He stood, looked up at us once more with a small smile and, as the band started up again, walked down the road and the procession continued on its journey through the square and back up to the church. So was this a psychic priest who had gathered the congregation together to come down Calle de Los Meridas to try and clear the vortex of energy for the benefit of the town? Of course not! It was an annual procession taking its normal route with three stops at temporary altars, one of which 'just happened' to be next to the convent. The roots of these processions and the various saints' days are pre-Christian.

I'm not a Catholic; the Catholic church doesn't teach us the truth. A lot of knowledge and information is kept from the people by the church. How wonderful it would be if everyone knew the whole truth. Yet the Catholic church does have some of the truth. Take the baptism ceremony when oil is anointed onto the baby. It is anointed onto the upper chakras yet the church does not teach knowledge of the chakras. Yoga philosophy teaches knowledge of the chakras. These are the seven energy centers that are not in the physical body but in the astral body.

The breaking of the bread and wine is an incredibly powerful ceremony. During the mass light pours down onto the altar. People who have full psychic ability have seen this happening. The bread and wine become imbued with light and when this is ingested the light permeates the aura of the recipient. So this ceremony does change people and make them more full of light, so as they leave church they are carriers of light. But so much is left untaught. How can anybody swallow the teaching of a single life deciding whether the soul will go to heaven or earth?

What the church does not teach is reincarnation. This is where the real meaning of an eye for an eye and a tooth for a tooth can be found. As you reap so shall you sow. If the congregation realized how true this was there would be no room for smugness. I thought about one of the nuns in the modern convent in Ugijar. (Ugijar still has an inhabited convent). She came to tell me not to talk to bad people. She was talking about the gypsies with their dark skin. Outwardly she looked like a wonderful soul, walking the streets in her nun's habits. Yet if her true outer garments, her aura, could be seen then, there would be no hiding the thoughts, feelings and her level of soul development.

Karalyn is not a Catholic, despite having been blessed by the Pope. She had taken an elderly lady friend of hers to Rome to see the Pope. As a lifelong church-going Catholic this had been her friend's dearest wish, to see the holy father of the Catholic church. As they stood in the crowds the Pope came towards them and, laying his hand on Karalyn's head, had given her a blessing.

CHAPTER FIFTEEN

June was here and with it came the hot weather. I was constantly slightly damp with perspiration. Although I tried to stay out of the sun, the odd occasion when I had been unable to avoid it had brought out my freckles. I had finally decided to rent a house in Ugijar for the summer. That way I would not have to spend my time driving up and down the mountain between Valor and Ugijar. I would also have hot running water, which I had not had in the apartment in Valor since before Christmas. I had found an old village house to rent in Ugijar, recently renovated and belonging to an English woman. Unfortunately it was unfurnished but as I was going to need furniture for the convent eventually, I didn't see that as a big problem. I didn't have any furniture so I would need to buy a bed just so that I would have somewhere to sleep. There were two furniture shops on the main road, neither of which looked huge.

"I'm looking for two beds," I told the shop owner. There were three models on display. "Is this all you have?" I asked.

"No of course not. Come with me."

I got into his car and I was driven a hundred yards to the other end of the main street. He unlocked a huge gate which opened onto a brick built warehouse and I followed him up an outdoor metal staircase to the first floor. I couldn't believe my eyes when he opened the door. This was a huge warehouse packed from floor to ceiling. There must have been at least a hundred different styles of mattress in there.

"Now, tell me what type of mattress you like. Do you want firm or soft, budget range or luxury, or in between?" he asked.

I picked out the mattresses I wanted and chose two bed bases.

"When do you want them delivered?"

"Now, if possible." It was half past seven and the shop shut at eight.

"No problem." He called his assistant who loaded up the van and within half an hour they were delivered to my door, taken to the rooms I pointed out, the flat-packed bases were assembled for me and the mattresses were unwrapped. That was what I call service. Not only that, I didn't have enough money on me to pay.

"Don't worry. Drop it into the shop tomorrow," they said.

As soon as the beds had been delivered I moved in to the house. I didn't have a fridge or an oven (who would put a brand new kitchen in with a hob but without an oven?) but I did have a toaster, so that would have to do for now. On that first day I was in the bedroom and I casually flicked on the light. The bedroom was reached by walking through two other connecting rooms and it didn't have a window, as was the norm in these old village houses.

I screamed as an almighty blue flash filled the room. It felt like a bomb blast. I tried the light switch upstairs and it snapped in half when I switched it on. Other than that nothing happened. However, whatever had caused the blue flash had left me without lights. Never mind, I would get it sorted out in the morning. I found some candles and lit them. In the morning I put a saucepan of water on the gas hob to boil and the bread in the toaster. There was a brilliant white flash and that was the end of the new toaster.

I contacted the English landlady who said she would send somebody round to look at the electrics. The builder who had renovated the property was supposed to have sorted out the wiring but he obviously hadn't. The electrician instantly condemned the existing fuse box and decided a new box was needed, and left me with no electricity and so I found myself living by candlelight.

The house may have been renovated but the workmanship was appalling. None of the internal doors closed. Nor did any of the windows, the consequence being that bugs and mosquitoes made a beeline for the house. The first night I slept there I hardly got a wink of sleep because I itched all night. It couldn't have been the bed or the bedding, I reasoned with myself because it was all brand new. When I got up in the morning I was covered from head to toe in bites. Huge hard lumps covered virtually every bit of skin, including my face, and the itching was sending me to the edge of sanity. The local chemist provided me with some cream, which didn't make the slightest bit of difference. The only relief I could get was from lying in a warm bath with a few drops of lavender oil in the water. Each bath took about an hour to run because the gas wall heater cut out every 20 seconds. I later found out this was due to an extremely dangerous split in the pipe. I was lucky I didn't blow up the house. Lying in the bath I counted 72 bites. Not a single part of my body had escaped the assault. Not only did they itch like crazy but I felt ill, as if the energy had been sucked from my body by these insects.

The house smelt bad as well. At first I thought the smell was coming from the neighbor's chickens which were true free range chickens as they lived in the garden next door. Or maybe it was the goat shed behind the house. I watched the goat herder bringing the goats home at sunset, guiding his herd into the half derelict building I overlooked from the patio. Goats had quite a sweet smell, so it couldn't be them. Gradually it dawned on me that the smell came from the ground floor bathroom. The bathroom was home to a few hundred flies, which emerged from the plug hole in the bath. I tried to keep the plug in at all times, which did help, but I suspected the real source of the smell was broken drains. The toilet had been wedged up against the wall so it was not possible to use it in a normal manner. It had to be sat on sideways. The stairs were enormous and extremely steep. Obviously there were no regulation measurements when this place was built.

The house was situated on the edge of town on a road that was too narrow for cars and it had been built on three floors. The bathroom was at street level, the three bedrooms were on the first floor and on the top floor was the kitchen and living room. This was the reason I agreed to rent the property – from here there were views of the spectacular red rock face and the few small farms, known as fincas, surrounded by agricultural land on which the local people grew their own vegetables and flowers.

I soon discovered I had the neighbors from hell. I had seen the two old men sitting on the street outside their house when I had gone to see about renting the place. I recognized them because I had seen them around town. These two brothers were never seen apart. The short man with only one eye always led the way. His brother followed behind, walking as quickly as his lame leg would allow him. He would take a step then drag his lame leg to catch up with his good leg. Every hundred yards or so he would stop and clear his nose, deftly hurtling the phlegm way to one side with his finger. His one-eyed brother would turn and look behind him to check that his lame brother was keeping up and if he wasn't he would hurl abuse at him. I soon realized that their rows were a daily occurrence. A friend translated one of their rows for me.

"You're a slut, you are." shouted the one eyed neighbour.

"How can I be a slut. I'm a man," came the reply.

"You're a man slut."

"There's no such thing as a man slut."

"Well there is now because you are one."

"I'm not."

"You are."

"Not."

"Are."

"I told you, I'm not."

"I told you, you are."

"Why am I a slut?"

"You just are. You were born that way."

Other topics for arguments included one brother accusing the other one of wearing his clothes or disagreements about what time to eat.

The narrow road outside the house was slippery with phlegm. The neighbor opposite shouted at the brothers on a regular basis and a couple of times a week she washed the road. The men were filthy. Their fingernails were black with dirt and their clothes were stiff with grime. I genuinely think that their clothes had never been washed as they did not have a washing machine nor anywhere to hang their clothes outside to dry. Fortunately I had a covered terrace which overlooked somebody's lovely garden. I never saw anyone in the garden so I would lie on my terrace and enjoy the warmth seeping into my bones. One day I was startled to see somebody just below me in the garden. It was Gabriel, he who was born in the convent. He was my other neighbor and the owner of the beautiful garden!

The delivery of the beds was watched with interest by the brothers, who spent all their waking hours outside their house, either leaning against the wall or slouched on the ground. It depended on the heat and how much they had had to drink. The more drunk they were, the louder the arguments. On the night of the full moon they had such a screaming argument that the lame brother lost his voice. Every time I opened the front door they were there, watching me. Every time I came home they were standing there, watching me. I always said hello but I had great difficulty in understanding anything they said.

I was not working at this time. There was no decent place to teach yoga. I was simply waiting for my new builder to finish his other jobs and start on mine. Patience. I was living off the money I had saved up to pay for the work so I hoped I didn't have to wait too long. It was good to have an English friend. Karalyn and I spent a lot of time walking Boo the dog, calling in the various bars to eat tapas. Boo loved to be taken for walks, anything to get out of the apartment. He hated the apartment and growled at things unseen. Whenever we returned from a walk Boo would pull back and had to be dragged inside. Objects were still being moved around and once Karalyn felt an invisible hand try to push her down the stairs. She also found pools of water on the floor which had no obvious source. Once she spotted a bare wire lying in one of these pools. I shudder to think what might have happened if she had stepped in it.

CHAPTER SIXTEEN

After a few months in the village house, I realized that I could not carry on living off my savings for much longer. I needed to go back to England and get a job because if I carried on living on the renovation money I wouldn't be able to afford the renovations. I had hoped that by now I would have my own apartment in the convent and a studio where I could teach yoga. But things had not gone smoothly. Tom seemed like a solid, dependable sort of person so I would be happy to let him get on with the work on the convent without me around.

The full moon was approaching, as was the summer solstice. I had a few loose ends to tie up before I flew back to England. I rang Tom to clarify the start date with him. I was wondering which day in August he might be able to start.

"Hilary, I've got some bad news for you. I didn't want to tell you when I last saw you because you were so ill with all those insect bites but the fact is that the ring beam your builders have put in is totally inadequate."

The ring beam is the reinforced cement wall that is built on top of the earth walls to take the weight of the terrace, which can be very heavy.

"It hasn't been built to match the architect's specs. Not that that matters because the architect's specs are wrong."

"So what can you do?" I asked.

"Well, we will have to completely undo the work that has been done already and start again from scratch. That'll add five to ten grand to the price of the work."

I groaned inwardly. But there was more.

"And looking at the earth walls, I notice that some of them are starting to bow and might have to be taken out."

Taking out a one meter thick earth wall is a major undertaking because of the amount of earth that has to be removed from the site.

"I'm not trying to bump up the price of the job but I just don't want you to get started on a project that is going to spiral out of control."

I told him I would need to think about it. I could not believe it. One blow after another. How much more could I take? More. When I bumped into Karalyn that morning she had news of my original builder, Miguel.

"He's in prison."

"What!"

"Yes, he's been done for fraud. He got involved with a woman who got pregnant by him and she took him to the cleaners. He was obsessed with her and wasn't seeing clearly. He was arrested part of the way through the job on the convent. That's why you didn't see him after a few weeks. He had been taken away."

So that's why he had disappeared. He hadn't even been to visit his sick mother in hospital and now I understood why. Was the policeman who turned up on the 11th November coming in search of Miguel? Is that why he hadn't turned up for work that day? Thank goodness I had found myself a good solid builder in Tom.

I left the cleaning and packing and wandered down the road for some fresh air. I walked up towards the main road. In the distance I could see the sky reddening as the sun started to set. The hills were glowing a deep crimson. Soon the almost full moon would rise. I heard a gentle tinkle of bells and watched as the goat herder guided his goats across the road with the help of a whip and his two dogs. He was old and wrinkled, deep nut brown, wearing a straw hat and eyed me admiringly with a gruff 'ola'. The goats crossed the road at the newly painted crossing, put in when the road was resurfaced a couple of weeks ago. Ugijar's first ever crossing. Goats would have been crossing this road for centuries just like today. I paused at the fountain for a cool drink of water and smelt the roses on the gentle breeze. It was a warm evening. Mothers were watching their children at play in the church square. There were no swings or slides. The children amused themselves playing hide and seek and running games, in perfect safety. A few people were sitting on the terrace at Carlo's bar. I overheard English, Dutch and German being spoken. More and more foreigners were starting to move into this part of Spain now.

I walked up towards the swimming pool bar. Ugijar, like most of the towns and villages, has a public outdoor swimming pool, which only opened during the summer months. Rico Santos was sitting alone at a small wooden table in the shade of the olive tree. I joined him. The pool was being prepared for opening. It was due to open the day after tomorrow, the day I was due to leave. Rico Santos was looking red-eyed. He explained that this month he has lost his mother, a cousin and two friends. He didn't know how much more he could take. The last death was on Sunday when his friend had died. His 38-year-old friend had had one drink too many and had lost consciousness. So they had taken him up to the 24-hour medical center in Ugijar where he was put on a drip. Five minutes later he died. Too much alcohol in his blood.

There was one more thing I needed do before I left for England. Karalyn and I had decided that we were going to try to dig a hole in the floor of the convent. If there were scrolls in there I would have to get them out before Tom moved in to start work. And if there weren't any then at least I would have tried to find them. There was nobody else in town that we could trust to help us. So we took our spades and started digging in the place where we both thought there was a stairwell. The earth was as hard as rock and after an hour we had barely made a dent in the floor. This was beyond us. We needed a pneumatic drill or something.

"It's no use. We're just not strong enough." Karalyn was exhausted. Her health was not good at the best of times and she didn't have a lot of stamina.

"I know. We will just have to leave it. I don't think anything wants to be found. The past is the past and that's where it can stay. Let's go and have a drink."

We walked down to a bar that recently opened. El Labrinto. Surely that translates as labyrinth?

An attractive young Spanish man was behind the bar. It was empty apart from him.

"A beer and an orange juice please."

He opened a beer and took half a dozen oranges from a beautiful, hand thrown ceramic bowl and started squeezing them. Fresh orange juice here was exactly that. Freshly squeezed.

"Why did you call your bar the Labyrinth?" I asked.

"I didn't call it that. It has always been called that."

It was a strange name for a bar because a labyrinth has mystical connections.

"Have you any idea why it's called that?"

"No, not really."

I wondered if this was a clue to the underground tunnel that the old gipsy had told me about. Maybe there was an entrance to a tunnel under this building somewhere. It was obvious the bar owner didn't know.

I decided to call in at the internet café on my way home to see what I could find out regarding labyrinths. Gabriel was leaning against the bar eating tapas.

"Heelaree!" he exclaimed. "Eat tapas with me".

I accepted the invitation and I was presented with a plate of bread and cheese drizzled with olive oil. I nibbled at the hard dry cheese, well matured and very tasty.

"Gabriel, do you know how much I want and need to see this book your family has?"

"Oh, but I have bad news for you. My sister cannot find it. She says she thinks it was lost when she moved house."

There comes a point when enough bad news leaves you immune to it. Of course I was disappointed but it seemed to me as if I was being given an overload of difficulty and I had got to the point where I could simply detach from it. Maybe this was all a lesson in detachment.

"Do you think she might find it one day?" I asked.

"This I do not know," he shrugged.

I didn't know either. So I let go of my need to see this book. If it was meant to appear it would. Just as if the scrolls were meant to be discovered, they would be. When my tapas was finished I booked an hour on a computer and spent some time on the internet. I found what I was looking for on a website called lessons4living.com.

'The Middle Ages showed a renewed interest in labyrinths and a design more complex than the classical seven-circuit labyrinth became popular. This was an eleven-circuit design divided into four quadrants. It was often found in Gothic Cathedrals but over time many of these eleven-circuit designs were destroyed or intentionally removed.'

Here was the number 11 making an appearance. The elusive 11. The 11 had been noticeable in my life because of its absence in recent weeks.

'The most famous of these remaining labyrinths is at Chartres Cathedral near Paris, France which was built around the year 1200. This labyrinth was meant to be walked but was reported to be infrequently used today. In the past it could be walked as a pilgrimage or for repentance. As a pilgrimage it was a questing, searching journey with the hope of becoming closer to God. When used for repentance, the pilgrims would walk on their knees. Sometimes this eleven-circuit labyrinth would serve as a substitute for an actual pilgrimage to Jerusalem and as a result came to be called the Road of Jerusalem. In walking the Chartres style labyrinth the walker meandered through each of the four quadrants several times before reaching the goal. An expectancy was created as to when the center would be reached. At the center was a rosette design which has a rich symbolic value including that of enlightenment. The four arms of the cross are readily visible

and provide significant Christian symbolism.'

So here was a reference to 11 circuit labyrinths. But why should they have been destroyed or intentionally removed from the cathedrals? Was there a message in them that the church did not want us to know? If the 11 circuit labyrinth could be substituted for a pilgrimage to Jerusalem, does the 11:11 also have a link to Jerusalem?

I had plenty of time to find out the answers to my questions because the time had come to leave Spain and go back to Bournemouth. I made one last visit to the convent before I left. As soon as I stepped through the heavy old front door I felt the change in energy. It was so different to the energy in the street. Although I was on my own, I knew that I was not alone. Despite having had the clearing ceremony with Sue, there was still the very strong feeling of being watched. I stood in silence in the cool, dark, entrance hall and listened. I could hear some sort of music coming from a distance. I tried to concentrate. It didn't sound like Spanish music, more like a deep slow chanting. Where was it coming from? I tried to locate the source, wandering through to the patio but it was definitely not coming from outside. I walked towards the broken window to the side of the property but it was even quieter over in that direction. It was still going, a quiet, persistent chanting of male voices. It was becoming quite loud now and it seemed to be at its loudest in the entrance hall. I opened the front door and looked outside. There was no music out in the street, just the quiet hum of small town life. I stepped back into the entrance hall and closed the door behind me. There it was again. It was a beautiful sound and I stood transfixed, as if the music had a trance-inducing ability. I don't know how long I had been standing there for, but I gradually realized that the sound was coming from beneath me. How could that be? There was no cellar. Suddenly, I remembered Karalyn mentioning the chanting monks that she had heard in her cellar. That's what it must be! As soon as I had this realization the chanting stopped and once more there was silence.

What was that about? Was this my final farewell from the convent? I stepped outside into the glaring sun. I was going back to England.

CHAPTER SEVENTEEN

In a way it was a relief to get back to Bournemouth. Back to my friends and family, the ability to easily understand snatches of conversation, 24 hour broadband wireless internet, a phone line, reliable hot water, fantastic shopping, English television and the public libraries. Yet I missed the beauty, the naturalness, and the slower way of life of Spain. I missed the fragrances, the dramatic colors and the way I would gasp in surprise at unexpected sights. I never gasped at the unexpected in Bournemouth.

I kept in touch with Karalyn via the internet. She had the key to the convent in her possession and was keeping an eye on the place for me. Tom was finishing another job and should be starting work on my project any day now. I was waiting to hear from him.

Then I received an email from Karalyn. *'Brace yourself. I have some bad news. Yesterday Tom had a horrific accident. He was driving a dumper truck when it overturned on him and crushed his spine. He is seriously ill in Granada hospital with total paralysis and they do not know if he will survive, which is ironic. Last week I woke in the night and felt compelled to go to the convent. The overwhelming message was leave it. Leave the convent alone. I think we have left it too long or there is too much stuff ever to make that place work. It's too much of a coincidence that that should happen to Tom just when he was about to start work on the convent. I don't know what to say but my gut feeling is to knock the place down and bury it all. I think there will only be misery. I think when we cleared it we cleared all the good stuff but I can't begin to tell you what it is like in there now. Truly evil. I went in there a week ago and felt a definite threat and I don't think I could go in there again. You have to trust this. There are so many coincidences with that place and maybe it will not be possible to uncover the truth. My feeling is to get rid of the place if you can.*

The convent is resisting giving up its secrets. Sorry to give you this bad news but I truly believe it should never happen now. Think about it and email me back as soon as possible. Much love Karalyn and boo xxxxxxxxx

I rang her immediately. She was at a fiesta and I could hear the music and the sound of people in the background. Images of my life in Spain came flooding back.

"How is he?" I asked.

"He's really bad. Can't feel a thing from the neck down and he can't move his head either. He is totally paralyzed and will never walk again. If he survives, that is. He has internal crush injuries which could prove fatal."

I was numbed by what I was hearing.

"How did it happen?"

"He was going down a steep track along the edge of a hill in the dumper truck and he went over the edge. He fell out of the truck and it landed on top of him, crushing him under the weight. It landed right on top of him. His friend Ian was working with him that day and rang for help immediately. He saw how badly injured Tom was and that they would have to act quickly. They brought in a helicopter and airlifted him to Granada hospital."

I was stunned. "I can't believe it. I spoke to him on Sunday and he said he was having a few days' holiday by the sea and then he should be able to start on the convent. He sounded so well and happy. He said he had worked hard all year and this was his first break. He was telling me how he would like to buy himself a place by the sea rather than up in the mountains in a few years' time. He would carry on working hard and build up a successful business. Now none of that is going to happen is it?"

I was beginning to think that this whole project was seriously jinxed. As soon as Anthony and I had been in the convent together we split up. My cousin lent me the money to buy the convent and then dropped down dead. My first builder ended up in prison. My next one was paralyzed, he might even lose his life. Following the clearing on the night of the full moon in May, Karalyn's flat became haunted. Sue's marriage ended within a month of the clearing. Typically, Karalyn read my mind.

"I think that place is evil," she said. "I don't know if we cleared all the good out of it when we did that ceremony and only left the bad in there, but that night last week when I had that sudden urge to go into the convent I experienced a terrible feeling of evil in there. Pure evil. That's the only way I can describe it. I went in there with Rico Santos. He tried to stop me but it was almost as if I was being possessed. I couldn't stop myself. We didn't stay long because the atmosphere was so unbearable. It's as if that convent had drawn me in with an invisible force."

I knew what she meant. It was a dark, clingy, cobwebby feeling. I had experienced it myself.

"When we got back to the flat the door was wide open again. Just like the time when I came back here after we had the clearing ceremony. Only this time I wasn't alone. This time I had Rico as a witness. I knew we had locked the door and no one else has a key. Rico Santos thought maybe someone had got in so he told me to keep back while he went to see. We stepped inside and the place was freezing cold even though it was a warm night. But then we both saw something out the corner of our eyes. Some sort of dark figure. Rico was deathly white. Shaking with fear. And then we saw that all the doors were open. All the internal doors, all the cupboard doors. Yet there are no other keys to the flat in existence.

Rico was totally spooked. He had never experienced something like this before in his life but he realized that what was happening in my flat was linked to the convent opposite. He knows a lot about the history of the convent and he told me that there used to be a tunnel between my place and the convent, which had been filled in."

I thought back to the times when Karalyn and I had heard the chanting coming from the cellar and I wondered if some monks had been trapped down there at some point. Why else would they have chosen the cellar as a place to sit and chant? Maybe they had even been locked in the cellar intentionally.

"It would be best just to knock the place down and forget about it," she said. "Walk away."

"It would be a shame" I said. "I would have loved to try and get those scrolls out. If I don't try again to find them then I would always wonder whether there was something hidden or not. Whether those past life memories were true or just my imagination. But maybe you're right. Maybe it is better just to cut my losses and walk away." It would certainly be a relief to get out. Out of Ugijar and out of the silent, dark clutches of the convent. "I'll think about it," I said, "and let you know."

I put the phone down and sighed. What had I got myself into? I thought about Rico Santos. He had kept offering me his heart when I had first arrived in town and I had rejected it. Yet there was a very strong connection between us and I knew that he must have had a part to play in that other life. I felt the same about Gabriel who had been born in the convent. I liked the fact that he was named after an angel in this life. I felt that same strong connection with him. I simply didn't know what part they played in that Knights Templar life.

What I did feel was a convergence of souls. It was as if we were a human key, each of us making up a part of the code. When all the souls were in place in Ugijar, then maybe then the convent would be able to reveal its secrets.

I felt so removed from everything now I was back in England. I was left not knowing what to do. What I wanted to was to just get on a plane and fly out to Spain there and then. But I had just got my yoga classes up and running and I knew I couldn't abandon my students. I trusted that everything would happen at the right time and maybe a delay was necessary.

Once I was physically removed from the convent and living the life of a householder I could see more clearly. It really was as if that place 'captured' me in a kind of dark, clinging spider's web when I was in Ugijar. With hundreds of kilometers between me and the convent I felt less tangled up in that web.

The 11:11 had drawn me to the convent but since I had got back from Spain it seemed to have disappeared from my life. I couldn't even remember when it had last appeared, it was so long ago.

I no longer had a builder and I could not wait another six months for yet another builder, a third one to start work because that convent would not survive another winter open to the elements. My cousin had died and I needed to pay the money back to his estate. I knew that I could not afford the renovations now so it was becoming obvious that the most sensible thing to do would be to sell up. That way I could pay off my debt and move forward in my life. If there were scrolls in there then I could accept that they would just have to stay buried. Either that or somebody else could find them. That's it. I had made my decision. It was definite. I was selling the convent.

I decided the next thing to do would be to go out to Spain, collect my few remaining belongings from the house in Ugijar and arrange with the local estate agent to put the convent up for sale. I searched the internet for the cheapest fare and booked my flight. It was only after I had booked my flight that I realized that my trip would coincide with the fiesta. One year on. One year older. A lot wiser.

I had never flown with this airline before. The take off was okay but as we neared our destination at Almeria airport it was obvious that we had hit a huge electric storm. The storm clouds were blackest clouds I had ever seen. I hoped it was not an omen. As we began our descent, the plane's engines began to make a strange noise, as if the engines were being revved up. The plane suddenly dropped like a stone then started to climb again. This happened several times. The final descent was erratic and much too fast. I have flown many times before so I know what a normal landing is like. This was not normal. We entered a dark cloud at high speed, flashes of lightning outside the window, and I glimpsed the runway below. We were going so fast that I knew we would never make it. We didn't.

Just after my glimpse of the runway a few meters below my window, the plane suddenly shot upwards. There was complete silence in the cabin as we climbed steadily skywards. It was as if we were one consciousness, united in this drama. The plane stopped climbing and started to circle the area. Round and round it went, for at least half an hour. Still nobody spoke. Even the children were silent. Finally we came in to land and there was a spontaneous cheer and a round of applause as we safely reached the tarmac. The tall, good-looking man sitting on my right spoke to the stewardess as we disembarked.

"What did she say?" I asked him as we walked across the runway towards the passport queue. Rainwater had gathered in huge puddles and was gushing in torrents down the side of the walkway.

"We overshot the runway," he replied.

"Is that all? I thought the engines made a strange noise."

"Yes, so do I. I think we might have been hit by lightning. That was a hell of a storm, wasn't it?"

"Awful! Did you feel the plane dropping like a stone?"

"Yes. We're lucky we made it."

I noticed a fire engine parked on the edge of the runway and wondered what had really happened. The pilot had given us no information at all during the descent or landing.

"Have you come to Almeria for a holiday?" the man asked.

"No. I've come to sell a property I own up in the mountains. An old Knights Templar church."

"Knights Templar?" His eyes widened. "Really? I'm mad on the Templars. I've got every book ever written on them. I've been studying them for most of my life. My name is a Templar name.

Gaudin. That's what sparked my interest in them. I'd love to see it."

And so it was that Kevyn came to visit Ugijar. Kevyn Gaudin. Another part of the human key to unlock the mystery.

He was staying on his friend's frigate moored in the recently built resort of Almerimar. I drove down to the coast the next day to collect him, bringing him up to Ugijar for the day to experience a taste of real Spain and to visit the convent. What a lot of knowledge he had. On entering Ugijar I had to park outside the town. The place was busy because of the fiesta. As we made our way through the packed market, we immediately bumped into Tim, the history teacher from Picena wearing his usual costume from the 1930s. I introduced Kevyn.

"Tim says that the Templars weren't in this area," I told Kevyn.

"Of course they were," said Kevyn.

"No. This area was occupied by the Moors during the time of the Templars" explained Tim. "So there weren't any Christians living in this area."

"Yes there were," replied Kevyn, "and the Templars were here too. They lived side by side, all sorts of religions. The Cabbalists, Jews, Templars, Muslims all living in harmony, sharing ideas and living in a world of tolerance. Anyway, the Templars were not Christians. They worshipped Baphomet."

Baphomet? Who was that? And the Cabbalists? This was news to me and immediately answered a question that had been puzzling me. I had seen a tiny church high up the mountain with a Star of David and a Christian cross on the top of its tower. The sign of the Cabbalists. That's what that was!

Tim looked angry. "Nonsense!" he said loudly. "This area was Moorish. And of course the Templars were Christian."

"No. They are thought to have originally formed to protect pilgrims entering Jerusalem. They protected the Christian pilgrims but they were not Christian as such," Kevyn asserted.

Jerusalem. It crossed my mind that I had thought maybe Jerusalem was linked to the 11:11 in some way. The Labyrinth link to Jerusalem. *'Walking the 11 circuit labyrinth counted as a pilgrimage to Jerusalem.'*

"Later, they formed a banking system which spread right across Europe," Kevyn continued. "They became very wealthy and successful. Until 1307. Then the Pope and the king of France decided they were heretics and hunted them all down. They existed for less than two centuries. Up until then they were granted all sorts of privileges and were looked upon favorably by the Holy See."

"The Holy See. Isn't that the Vatican?" I asked.

"Yes. They had the support of the Pope until 1307."

"Even though they weren't Catholics?"

"Yes. There's a lot of mystery surrounding the Templars. Nobody really knows the truth. In the end the Pope and the king of France decided to wipe them out. They were accused of worshipping the head of John the Baptist and spitting on the cross."

That was strange thing for him to say. I had heard that spitting on the cross was part of one of the highest initiations of the Masonic movement. If the initiate refused to spit on the cross they were told that they had done the right thing, but they would never reach the highest degree (the 33rd degree). If they did spit on the cross they proved their loyalty to the order, above their loyalty to Christ, so they could reach the highest degree.

And here was mention of John the Baptist again. He was appearing far too often for it to be coincidental.

We parted company with Tim before his blood pressure reached boiling point.

"Is he Catholic?" asked Kevyn, once we were out of earshot.

"Why do you say that?"

"Because I can hear that he has been heavily indoctrinated. Some people never learn to challenge what they have been told."

We reached the convent. As soon as Kevyn saw the carved door he recognized the carving of the double-headed eagle.

"What a fantastic door, That's so typically Knight Templar," he said.

"Tim thought it was House of Hanover."

"No way!"

He suddenly shuddered.

"My god, this place is thick with atmosphere, isn't it?"

I had to agree. It was thick with darkness.

"There's a nun here." Kevyn was looking beyond me towards something I could not see. He closed his eyes and appeared to be concentrating.

"She was 17 when she was killed," he continued. "Killed by Arabs because she was Christian. She resides here in the convent. She doesn't want to leave."

Kevyn went quiet again as if he was tuning in.

"Seven females were killed here. One was only six years old. Killed by a sword or a knife. Stabbed, but not raped. The whole village was attacked."

Kevyn shook his head slowly from side to side. I certainly hadn't been expecting this. I had brought Kevyn up to Ugijar because he was strong and muscular, with a view to digging. As a former member of the armed forces he was much fitter than an average Englishman. So it came as a surprise to me to discover that he was currently training to be a remote viewer.

Kevyn had first come across remote viewing whilst he was in the army. In fact the CIA and the US army thought highly enough of remote viewing to spend millions of taxpayers' dollars on research in a program referred to as Stargate. Remote viewing is the alleged psychic ability to perceive places, persons and actions that are not within the range of the senses. Remote viewing could be called psychic dowsing. Instead of a twig or other device, one uses psychic faculties to dowse the entire galaxy, if need be, for whatever one wants to find: oil, water, buried treasure, a lost child, a buried body, a hostage site thousands of miles away, or to see inside the Pentagon or the Kremlin. I would explain remote viewing as the ability to travel in ones astral body in full consciousness. Normally we are not conscious when we are in our astral body. We call that state being asleep!

I recalled my cousin John being famous for his dowsing ability. He had often been asked to find water sources on isolated properties in the area of England where he had lived.

Wandering around the convent it soon became clear that all the rainwater that had poured into the earth walls had seriously damaged them. They were crumbling, huge piles of earth and pottery lying on the floors. They had gone past the point of repair and were so seriously weakened that I knew I now had no choice. The convent would have to be demolished.

We were standing in the room where I thought the stairs to the tunnel used to be.

"There's stuff hidden here you know," Kevyn said.

Here we go again....

"Yes."

"Scrolls."

He was the fifth person to say that. I now knew for certain that there must scrolls hidden in this ancient building. I could walk away from it now. I had become so detached that, although I knew for certain that under these floors lay some historic documents, I trusted the universe so much that I knew that if they needed to be found, they would be found. I also knew it probably wouldn't be me that found them. Now that the convent could not be restored, it was bound to be demolished. When something was built in its place they would have to dig some seriously deep foundations...

After our visit to the convent I called in at the estate agents to arrange to put the place up for sale. It felt right to do this. I was following my intuition rather than signs by making this decision. It was midday, the bells were ringing as I opened the door. Emily-Anne, the bilingual assistant estate agent, was sitting at her desk. I explained that I was moving back to England and wanted to sell up. As we talked, our conversation moved on to astrology and the fact that I was an astrologer.

"I'm a Scorpio," she told me.

"Were you born in October or November?"

"November."

"What date?"

"The 11th. I was born on the 11th of the 11th, Armistice day."

Here was my sign, the confirmation that I was doing the right thing. On this five day trip to Spain I had had a brush with death on the flight over, I had met a Knights Templar expert on the plane who was also a remote viewer and a natural psychic (what are the chances of that?), and now I had met someone in Ugijar born on 11:11 just as the church bells were ringing midday. I was going to sell the convent and get out of Ugijar. And I was never coming back. The sooner I released myself from this place the better. I had got to the point where I couldn't wait to walk away and leave it all behind.

CHAPTER EIGHTEEN

It was April, almost nine months since I had left Spain. The convent remained unsold and quite frankly I was baffled. I would have thought that with all this attention on the Knights Templars thanks to the Da Vinci code that people would have been queuing up to buy a piece of real life history and mystery. Especially as the convent was on the market for the modest sum of 150,000 euros. I just didn't understand.

When I don't understand something and can't work it out in my head, there is only one thing to do. I meditate on the matter. So I sat silently upright on my chair and brought the attention to my breath. I silently asked 'What do I need to do to get things moving?' Then I sat and waited. The answer came as a thought. 'Maybe I need to dig for the scrolls.'

Was this why things were at a stalemate? Did I need to get somebody in to look for the scrolls before the convent would release me from its dark, tangled grip?

I thought about the past life memory I had had where I was sweeping down a staircase with a metal casket. There were two visions that were quite closely intertwined and it was difficult to separate the memories of the two lives. In both lives I had hidden things near the point of death, once it was scrolls and once it was some objects that I did not want anybody to find. Both times I was pursued at the point of death and in at least one of these lives I was tortured then beheaded. In one life, I was a well-built man and in the other life I had a much finer body. More than that I cannot say. At least I knew for certain that I would not be living in the convent for a third time in this life. I was never going back to live in Ugijar.

I emailed Karalyn with my insights on the convent.

'Hi Karalyn

I have been thinking about the convent. I don't think the convent will release me until I have tried to look for the buried scrolls. You and I both think they are in that back room. If we are right, then there are some stairs under the floor in that place where we tried to dig. I was thinking of paying someone to go and dig up the floor – just for a few hours or a day at most – to see if they come across some stairs. If they do find stairs, then we could well be right about our past life memories. If they don't find any then I will doubt the whole past life thing. Because of our strong past life connection, we are tied to the convent, both of us. Maybe this is why your place has not sold as well? Would you be able to get someone in for a day and sell my car to pay them? It needs to be kept quiet! Though I don't know if that is possible in Ugijar!

Hope you are well, lots of love Hilary xxxxxxxxxxxxx'

Her reply followed a couple of days later.

'Hi Hilary, it's so strange you have said this. I have been thinking this also. Rico Santos as well said out of the blue that we need to dig in there. He won't say anything, he is not trusting of the church but he knows there is a tunnel which he says goes to the medical center, so we will do a few test drills and if the tunnel is there we will find it. I will let you know how the dig goes. How much time do we have? I will be in touch soon love karalyn and boo xxxxx'

'Hi Karalyn

Keep me closely posted on the search for stairs. You know where I think they are.

The convent has not sold so we have some time to search.

The fact that you were thinking along the same lines as me is a really good sign.

I just wonder what part Rico Santos played in that previous life! Hxxxxxxxxxxxx'

I felt pleased that something was happening, that there was some movement regarding the convent. I was quite excited. Even if no stairs were found, at least we would know that we had tried. I relaxed about the whole thing, leaving it in Karalyn's capable hands.

The next day, completely out of the blue, my friend Catherine emailed me. I hadn't heard from her for ages. She had been spending a lot of time in her apartment in India.

'Hi Hilary, I am back in Wales now and feel the need to connect with you quite urgently but I can't find your phone number. Please could you ring me when you get this and leave your number on my answer phone. Speak to you soon. love Catherinee xxxxxxx'

Catherine is my only psychic friend. I'm not normally surrounded by psychic people. It was only in Spain that I found myself in the strange world of psychic people. My friends in England were mostly other yoga teachers and college lecturers. Except for Catherine. She was a natural psychic and in the past she had worked on stage, picking people from the audience and giving them messages from their deceased friends and relatives.

Her psychic abilities were phenomenal. She was sitting in my home in Bournemouth one day when she suddenly began to pull at her ear, in exactly the same way as my late father used to. She then announced that she had a message from my father. As my father had lain dying from cancer, I had told him to follow the bright light as he died and he would be met on the other side by friends and family that he had known and who had passed on.

"He says he wants to tell you that it was exactly like you said it would be. He crossed over and was met by friends and family. Does that make sense to you?"

"Yes Catherine. I know exactly what he means. Thanks!"

So why should Catherine suddenly want to get in touch with me urgently after months of silence? I needed to ring her to find out.

"Hi Catherine, it's Hilary. I got your email."

"Good," she replied. "I'm glad you got back to me so quickly. I felt this urgent need to connect with you but I don't know why. What's going on with you at the moment?"

I explained what was happening at the convent, and the fact that digging was about to commence.

"You need to contact Sabberan," Catherine stated. She said it in such a way that it was a command rather than a suggestion. Sabberan was a clairvoyant and healer who specialised in space clearing. I felt a sort of prickly sensation on my skin that I usually got when something important was being communicated to me.

"He gets dozens of calls a week," she said. "You need to leave as many details as possible. Mention the fact that it was once a Knights Templar church and mention the curse."

I had not thought about the convent being cursed until that moment. It was apparent that it was a spooky and unfortunate place, but did she think it had a curse on it? Did Catherine know more than she was letting on?

"Ok. I'll contact him in the morning," I agreed.

The next morning I connected to the internet and found Sabberan's web site. He gives readings by telephone so his number was there. I thought about the message I wanted to leave on his answer phone. I would need to say enough to catch his attention but I didn't want to ramble on, so I made a few notes.

Knights Templars / major occult activity / accidents and death / my name and phone number / Catherine recommended him.

I dialled, a few rings…

A man's voice answered. "Hello."

"Oh hello. I wanted to speak to Shabberan."

"Shabdan speaking."

This was the last thing I had expected. Shabberan had answered the phone himself.

"Oh good. I need to speak to you. I need your help. Catherine Radding recommended I get in touch with you. Do you know Catherine?

"I probably do," replied Shabberan. "But I meet so many hundreds of people in my work that I can't remember her. Anyway, that's not important. You have found your way to my door so I am sure I can help. Please explain briefly what it is you need help with."

How on earth could I explain the last two years briefly? I did my best.

"I bought an old Knights Templar church."

"Knights Templar?"

I could hear instantly by the tone of Sabberan's voice that he was interested.

"Yes. I bought it as an old convent but I subsequently discovered that it was a former Knights Templar place. But once I bought it, really bad things started to happen. The person who put up the money died suddenly. The builder had a terrible accident and is now paralyzed." I didn't elaborate any further.

"What were you going to use the convent for?" asked Sabberan.

"A yoga center."

"Where is it?"

"In Ugijar, in the Alpujarra mountains."

"Wait a minute."

There was a short silence before Sabberan spoke again. I guessed he was tuning in to something, either the building or his guides.

"It could be a decoy light center."

What's that?" I asked.

"A center that draws in the light like moths to a candle flame. But actually draws people to a dark place. I came across this once before in Devon. Hold on."

Again the line went silent. Several minutes passed before he spoke again.

"There is an artery into the earth. It's like a bleed valve, a bleed valve into the earth to release dark energies. The dark energies are stored there. They're imprisoned."

I wasn't sure I understood what he meant. I remembered Psychic Sue mentioning the vortex of negative energy and I wondered if he was referring to the same thing.

"This is something we are to work on together. You have been led to this place to clear the darkness that is there. You have made good decisions about the convent so far, excellent choices. Now it is time to start the clearing. Are you comfortable with this, Hilary?"

I replied that I was. In fact my vision of the convent had been that of a grid of light around the earth with a serious blockage at the site of the convent. I knew deep inside that I was being sent to unblock the grid, it was just that in my ignorance I hadn't realized what exactly that entailed. I hadn't thought through the process of releasing darkness, what would actually happen when darkness was released into the physical universe.

"The Guardians of Light will help us with this work."

As soon as Sabberan said that, I went all goosepimply again. This felt right. Forget the signs. My intuition said this was right and to me that was the most important thing.

"They are here now. But we need to arrange a time when we can meet. I am going to give this priority because I think it's important. How about next Tuesday?"

"But I live on the south coast of England!" Sabberan lived north of Dundee in Scotland. It's hundreds of miles away, almost the opposite end of Britain.

"Time and space are irrelevant with this type of work," he said. "We will make contact by phone and begin the necessary work of clearing the darkness from this site."

I suddenly remembered that Karalyn was trying to arrange for somebody to start to dig.

"My friend is about to start digging up the floor. Do you think it's okay to go ahead with that?"

"Digging? What for?"

"Well I have been told that there is something hidden there. Several people have told me."

"Treasure?"

"No. Scrolls."

"Scrolls? What sort of scrolls?"

"I'm not sure. The word scrolls has come up a few times so I had to take notice."

"Don't dig. Wait until we have had our meeting so that I am clearer about the whole situation. We need to be clear about what needs to be done. Phone me on Tuesday at one thirty."

"Ok, Sabberan. Thanks."

After I put the phone down I emailed Psychic Sue to ask whether a negative vortex of energy was the same as a bleed valve for negative energy. She replied that it was.

I began to think about all the things that had happened since I first stepped into the convent. Could there be a curse on the place?

The first thing that happened was that I broke up with my fiancé after a five-year relationship. Then my flat was sold, only for the sale to fall through at the very last minute, leaving me in a position where I could lose my substantial deposit. My cousin stepped in and helped me out with 70,000 euros, only to drop down dead suddenly a few weeks later. My first builder was sent to prison days after removing the roof of the convent. Then Karalyn entered the building with me and two weeks later her 20 year marriage ended. Her boyfriend Rico Santos worked on the convent and his mother died within weeks, rapidly followed by three other friends and relatives. Psychic Sue came to dowse and within weeks, she was separated from her husband. Shortly afterwards her newly acquired home and retreat center was sold. Tom the builder came to give me a quote and within a week of the proposed start date he had a terrible accident, almost died and was now paralyzed. Was this all coincidental or was there a curse on the convent as Catherine had hinted?

I definitely felt as though I was embroiled in something peculiar. All this seemed to have stemmed from my leap of faith which I had taken when I had made an offer on the convent because of the coincidences, especially the 11:11. If I had ignored the 11:11 I would probably have had a nice little yoga center by now because I would have bought a more realistic, smaller project. I tried not to let myself be sidetracked by thoughts like these. 'What ifs' were a waste of time. Only 'what is' matters.

I contacted Karalyn and told her to hold fire on the digging. She informed me that her boyfriend Rico Santos had managed to get hold of a pneumatic drill but they would wait for the okay from me.

CHAPTER NINETEEN

Daily life was mundane. I had the washing to do, the shopping, the cleaning, paying the bills, weeding the garden. Yet I had this other dimension to my life, the life of signs and coincidences. I could share my mundane life with people because they could identify and empathize with it. But my 11:11 life was shared by very few people.

Sitting at my computer one morning, I had an idea. I simply put 11 11 into the search engine on the computer to see what would come up.

Armistice day. 11/11 at 11am.

Childline, a help line for children tel 0800 11 11

11.be. A Dutch site about unions and coalition groups.

9/11 and the twin towers. 9/11 had come up even though I had put in 11 11.

I pictured the twin towers and it struck me that side by side, they had written the number 11 on the New York landscape. A great big number 11, constructed from glass and concrete! I knew that New York was the eleventh state of America. So I put 9.11 into the search engine. That brought up loads of sites. And loads of very interesting information.

· The first plane to hit the tower was flight 11.

· There were 92 people on board (9+2=11).

· The second plane had 65 people on board. (6+5=11).

· The destruction of the towers took place on 11th September, or 9/11 as it is now known. (9+1+1=11).

· 911 is the phone number for the emergency services in New York.

· The total number of victims in the hijacked planes was 254. (2+5+4=11).

· September 11 2003 was day number 254 of the calendar year. (2 + 5 + 4 = 11)

· The Madrid bombing took place on 3/11/2004. (3 + 1 + 1 + 2 +

4 = 11).

· The tragedy of Madrid happened 911 days after the Twin Towers incident. (9+1+1=11).

But what the hell did 9/11 have to do with the convent? Lots of elevens were appearing, but I decided I was getting sidetracked and went back to my 11 11 search.

K is the eleventh letter of the alphabet. Katarina, the estate agent who found the convent... Karalyn, who had been with me in the convent in a previous life. Kevyn, who had spent his life researching the Knights Templars.

Yes. But there were other people whose names did not begin with K, I reasoned, such as Psychic Sue and Gabriel.

I scrolled down the findings of the search engine. Nothing interesting came up. So I added the word coincidence. '11 11 coincidence.'

Immediately an interesting site appeared, all about 11:11 and coincidence. I read through it and sure enough there were other people experiencing the 11:11 phenomena. But there was nothing to explain what it is or why it is happening other than the information that it was a wake up call. Where was all this leading? It must be leading to something or what was the point? Yes, sure, there were lots of elevens in my life but why?

It was April 4th. At 2pm I phoned Sabberan as arranged. He had a bad cold.

"I'm human just like you," he reasoned.

He was born Martyn Jones but had adopted the name Sabberan as this is his spiritual name. So, like the rest of us, he was a spiritual being in a human body. He claimed to be Lord Ajnu, the Keeper of the Keys.

"I have been tuning in to the convent. But first I need to tell you about my discovery of the River of Light. Have you heard of it?"

"No. Tell me about it."

"The River of Light is a layered energy that surrounds the Earth that can be likened to an aura around the world."

"You mean like an aura that people have around them?"

I knew about auras because of my yoga studies. According to yoga we are not just a physical body. We have a 'subtle' body which consists of a network of channels called 'nadis'. They are a bit like veins. Life force (prana) flows through these channels in the same way as blood flows through veins. The purpose of yoga is to clear these channels so that the energy can flow freely. Free flowing energy leads to better health and higher states of consciousness. The most important of these channels is the one that runs from the base of the spine to the top of the head. It is along this channel that the chakras are situated. They're like junction boxes. The whole body gives off an aura, according to the state of your 'nadis' and chakras. The more life force you have running through your channels, the brighter and clearer your aura.

So yes, the River of Light could be seen as an aura.

"This amazing energy has only just been discovered," he explained. "Layered like the auric field around the human body it possesses light bodies beginning with the etheric, emotional, lower mental, higher mental and on towards Source."

"What do you mean by Source?"

"I mean the Source of all that exists. Some people might say God. Or Light. They say that no life could be sustained in manifested Creation without the River of Light Consciousness Stream."

"I can understand this because the yoga texts state that something called prana permeates everything and nothing could exist without it."

"That's right. And the Chinese call it Chi."

"Chi is what acupuncture works with isn't it?" I asked.

"Well the lower layers of this River of Light are 'polluted'" continued Sabberan. "Viewed psychically, the etheric body shows murky muted colours which vary over the different continents. Some places are more clogged and dark than others. A lot of the places around the Med and North Africa are quite dense."

"What about Ugijar?"

"Huge mountains, land masses such as the Sierra Nevada are capable of holding lots of energy."

"So this area is clogged at the etheric level, the level that can't be seen?"

"Yes. And the convent is actually a bleed valve for negative energies, as I told you last time."

Trust me to go and buy a bleed valve.

"This consciousness stream can be cleansed and re-aligned to Source allowing a powerful stream of higher consciousness to pervade the whole world," Sabberan concluded. "Is this making sense to you?"

"Yes. It sounds very similar to a vision I had a few months ago. Only I called it a grid of light."

This did indeed correspond to exactly to what I had discovered, that the grid was blocked in the area of the convent, a bit like a blocked drain. A load of gunge was preventing the flow of light.

"So what can we do about it?" I asked.

"We need to clear it. The convent can be compared to a festering wound that needs to be lanced. Things might get worse before they get better but it would be better to release the poison quickly. We can do that now if that feels okay to you."

I liked the way that Sabberan asked for my permission before he went ahead with anything, though I couldn't imagine how things could get any worse.

"Yes, that's fine by me. But what do I have to do?"

"Just tune in. Stand with your feet firmly planted to the floor."

So there I stood in my living room, me on one end of the phone and Sabberan on the other. I stood there in silence, aware of my breathing. Standing still and waiting. I didn't know what I was waiting for. Then Sabberan spoke.

"The Guardians of Light have appeared at the convent."

I immediately broke out in goosepimples but I didn't know why. Nor did I understand how he could see what was there at the convent. It must have been by remote viewing.

"We ask to clear the site under grace, with help from our guides."

I remained standing and suddenly my neck clicked, a huge release in the left side where I had had such problems on my arrival in Ugijar.

"I am Lord Anju, Keeper of the Keys. I work on the purest vibration so every key is available to me." Sabberan was saying.

As soon as I heard these words I thought of the huge ancient key that opens the door of the convent. The same key that I would have held in my hands many times in past lifetimes. The key that felt so familiar to me when I first took hold of it that hot August day in Ugijar.

"The language of light will open this aperture. I am going to open this aperture now. Stay with me Hilary," continued Sabberan.

Then he started to speak in a strange language. Yet it sounded familiar, as if I had known and understood these words in the past. I cannot repeat the words he spoke here for I know it is a sacred language and the words have incredible power. These words must remain secret for now. For several minutes the chant or prayer continued. Then I heard Sabberan thanking people. He was having a conversation with beings I could neither see nor hear.

"Yes, yes. Blessings to you too. And thanks. Many thanks. Blessings. I will, I will." Then he spoke to me. "Hilary. The wound has been lanced and the healing has begun. Are you okay?"

"Yes, but my neck gave a mighty click during that."

"Your guides were here. You have some very powerful guides assisting you in this life. They are very brave. They are both courageous and focused."

I had heard about guides before. I had never seen a guide but the idea made sense to me. "What do we do now? Can I tell my friends to go ahead and dig?"

I really needed to sell that convent because I had to pay back the money to my late cousin's estate so I was getting impatient. Impatience was one of the issues I was working on in this life.

"No," he said firmly. "The 'wound' is wide open. You can't go disturbing things at this point. We will talk again in a few weeks and see how things are progressing. Call me in three weeks."

"Ok, Sabberan. Thanks for your help."

The next morning my phone bill arrived. It was for eleven pounds and eleven pence. I set off for the supermarket to pick up some groceries and when I arrived I parked the car. Just as I was about to turn off the engine the CD came to an end. I looked at the trip meter. It was 333. I laughed. Maybe I was having a repeated numerals day. When it came to paying for my shopping I discovered I had chosen a very slow queue. The cashier pressed a button for assistance and a light above her started to flash, illuminating her till number. Number 11. So I stood there under a flashing 11and glancing at my digital watch I realised the time was 11:11. The price of my shopping was eight pounds, eighty nine pence. Just two eights, not three? But I realised why when I saw the till. I had handed over a twenty pound note to pay and my change was eleven pounds eleven pence!

Even in the world that I call the mundane world, I sometimes experienced this magic. Then the 11:11 would disappear for a while. Some days it was everywhere, some days it was not there at all. Where was it leading? Where was it coming from? I had so many questions but so few answers.

Another email came from Karalyn.

'Hi Hilary

There is lots happening in the convent at the moment, the walls inside are just crumbling, the shell doesn't look too bad but the soil is pouring out of the walls and more of the upstairs is collapsing. It's almost as if it's dying, or angry. I was worried it might just collapse but Rico Santos does not think the whole building will go, just the insides, but I would try to sell it quick, he is going to ask other people if they might be interested. We have had more terrible storms last two days. I looked out of my window and saw a jagged flash of lightning over the convent. I think it might have been hit. It was very spooky. There are more storms to come. Whatever is in there it doesn't want to be discovered all this has happened since the light workers started. More than a coincidence I think. I will keep you posted. love karalyn and boo xxxxxxxxxx'

It certainly sounded like the convent was dying and I thought Karalyn was correct to link it to the work that Sabberan was doing. Three weeks later I contacted Sabberan again for a progress report.

" So...the convent."

"Yes. Has there been any progress?" I asked.

"I tuned into the energy in the convent last night and it's much clearer. But it is linked to some other sites in the Mediterranean which are not clear and which are affecting it.

There is an underground connection to other sites, extending to the south of France, Italy, parts of Egypt and North Africa," explained Sabberan.

"Is it clear enough to dig?"

"Unfortunately, no. I know you want to get things moving but it is just too dangerous to disturb the place right now. I need to do some more clearing. The work is not yet complete. I'm sorry but you'll have to wait. I need to spend time working on those sites and clearing the Mediterranean basin."

Waiting seemed to be the key word for my life right now. It was all I ever seemed to do.

"When they are clear, will I be able to dig?"

"Yes. The work has been started, so we will just have to wait until it's finished. Have you heard anything from the convent?" he asked.

"Yes I have. Shortly after the healing work had started, there were violent electric storms in Ugijar. My friend looked out of her window and saw huge flashes of lightning directly above the convent."

"I wonder if it was hit."

"So do I. She said an inside wall had fallen down after the storms."

"That's okay. You don't need to worry because the place is protected and already it is much clearer. Such a shift has taken place. What I'll do is work on the connecting sites. When is the dark of the moon?"

"The new moon is tomorrow evening."

"Perfect. I'll ring you after the weekend."

After the weekend, Sabberan phoned me. This time he was much more positive. He told me that the energy in the convent was now flowing freely. The angry energy that had been there had gone. He said that there were nineteen energy sites directly linked to the convent, sites as far away as Rome, Yugoslavia, Italy, Israel, Tunisia, Egypt and southern France.

"And they've all been cleared?"

"Yes. The whole area is much lighter and clearer there now."

I hardly dared ask if the digging could begin at last.

"Yes. It will be safe to dig now. Are you going over to Spain?"

"No, I can't."

"Who is going to dig then?" he asked. "Can you give me their names so I can tune into their energies?"

"Karalyn."

"Hold on."

Sabberan tuned into her energy field.

"Yes. That's fine. Who else?"

"Rico Santos, sometimes known as Chispar."

Before Sabberan even spoke, I knew it was not going to be okay. It's hard to explain what I felt, other than it felt like a huge, overwhelming, NO reverberating through my being.

"It's not ok," said Sabberan. "There's a problem with Rico's energy. Hold on."

There was a pause before he continued.

"It links back to the Inquisition."

The odd thing is that the moment Sabberan said that word, I instantly knew the whole scenario surrounding Rico Santos in that previous life. I knew that he was not one of us, that he had been responsible for my death and Karalyn's too. And I found it quite odd when I thought back to the way that he and I had connected so strongly when I had first arrived in Ugijar. Now he and Karalyn were living together as a couple in a strong but stormy relationship.

"Does that make any sense to you?" asked Sabberan.

"Yes. It does."

"If Rico Santos digs in his current state he could release another hex."

"Hex? What's a hex?"

"A curse."

There was that word again. A curse.

"What can we do? I don't know anyone else who could dig."

"Well I can work on his energy, but I'd need his permission. Do you think he would be willing?"

"I'm not sure. He doesn't speak any English at all so I don't know how you'd communicate with him."

"I won't need to speak to him. I can do the work remotely."

"Okay. I'll contact Karalyn and ask her."

Hi Karalyn

I have just had a session with Sabberan who says that the energy in the convent is now flowing. It is not completely clear, but should be safe to dig in a few days. Except for one thing ... Rico Santos cannot go ahead and dig in his current state. Sabberan believes that the energy working through Rico Santos is linked to the times of the

Spanish Inquisition. Didn't I say to you a few emails ago, that I didn't know what part Rico Santos had to play in this scenario but that I would find out when the time was right? Well, I think we've found out.

Anyway, it won't be a problem if his energy is sorted, but Sabberan cannot work on Rico Santos's energy field without his permission. Could you talk to Rico Santos and ask him if he gives permission. It is up to you how much of the truth you reveal to him.

Sabberan can do the work from where he lives in Scotland, he doesn't have to meet either of you. But whatever happens, don't start to dig until I give the go ahead or more curses could be released.

Don't panic about any of this. I think we are finally coming to completion.

Lots of love Hxxxxxxxxxxxxxxxxxxxxxxxx'

A week passed and there was no response from Karalyn. How was she going to get this message across to Rico? "Oh by the way Rico, you're energy is in a bad way and you killed me and Hilary in a previous life." I didn't think that would go down well. Maybe he was not going to give permission, which would mean I would have to find somebody else to dig? All I could do was wait.

CHAPTER TWENTY

So, according to Sabberan, my convent was linked to places as far away as Egypt and Israel. I knew that Ugijar had a long and ancient history but now I was beginning to wonder just how far back in time the history of this town went. Ugijar and the surrounding areas have been inhabited since the Neolithic age. The Phoenicians, Greeks, Carthaginians, Romans and Moors had all established themselves in this area at various times in history.

As it was the number 11:11 that had brought me to Ugijar, I began to wonder if there was any connection between Ellingham in Dorset, England and Ugijar. Ellingham is where I had experienced the 11:11 day that frightened me, when the car milometer and the bible and the time were all at 11:11. I decided to take a trip out to Ellingham church to see if I could shed any light on its history. I was sure I had seen an information pamphlet for sale in the church the last time I was there. I needed to call in at the nearest supermarket to fill up on petrol on the way. As soon as I had filled the tank I set the trip meter at zero so I could keep an eye on my fuel consumption. I made a mental note not to buy another car with such a powerful, thirsty engine.

The drive to Ellingham was only about 15 minutes from my home in Bournemouth. I turned off the main road, drove along the narrow country lane and pulled up outside the church. There was nobody around and it was raining so I sat in the car and waited for the rain to ease off a bit. I had parked right in front of the churchyard wall and as I sat looking at it I could see some ancient pieces of carved stone incorporated into the wall. Were these carved stones part of an older building that had once sat on this site? I was sure they must be. It was one o'clock. 1.01pm. The trip meter in the car read 111. So it was obviously exactly 11.1 miles exactly from the petrol station to the church. Ellingham was still working its magic for me. But I didn't feel frightened this time. I simply smiled to myself and made a dash for the church door in an effort to avoid the rain.

I found the history pamphlet. The church as it stood today dated from the thirteenth century though there must have been an earlier one on the same site as the church as Ellingham was mentioned in a Charter of 1160, which was in the hands of Eton College, England. Originally Ellingham was a cell of an Alien Benedictine Priory. An Alien priory is one which is foreign, normally French. That means that a group of Benedictine monks, most of whom were probably French, were living deep in the Hampshire countryside of England. Even if they were not all French, their superiors certainly would have been.

But where was the link from Ellingham to Ugijar and therefore to the Knights Templars? As the convent in Ugijar was originally Templar and Ellingham was Benedictine, could there be a link between the Templars and the Benedictines?

I did some research on the internet and discovered a few things of particular interest. Templar rule was based on the rule of Saint Benedict and their motto is also thought to have been Benedictine in origin. The Benedictines were formed in the sixth century, long before the Templars who were first mentioned early in the twelfth century. So did the Templars actually grow out of the Benedictine movement?

After the king of France issued his order to destroy the Knights Templars, a small Benedictine Monastery near Weissenbourg, France, protected the Templars. Did they help them to escape with their treasure, whatever that was?

It was 11th May when I made another discovery. The *Da Vinci Code* fever was hotting up because the film of the book was about to be released. On the evening of May 10th there were several programs scheduled about the Da Vinci code so I decided to watch television and see if I could glean any new information on it. One of the programs talked about how sites of some of the old Knights Templar churches were accurately aligned to form a pentagram when they were drawn on the map. Did the convent, or Ellingham form a pentagram with anything?

I would need to find out. My starting point was the old church in Ellingham where my 11:11 journey had started. I got out the map and covered it with greaseproof paper as I didn't have any tracing paper in the house. I made a mark with my felt tip on Ellingham. Now what? I didn't know how to draw a pentagram. I hated maths at school and gave it up at the first opportunity so I was virtually mathematically illiterate. I looked at the places near to Ellingham that I knew and had visited and I could see that Shaftesbury was not that far from Ellingham. Taking my long ruler, I drew a line from Ellingham to Shaftesbury. Extending the line further it went through Glastonbury. It was not just near the line but it was an exact alignment. That was interesting, as legend said that Glastonbury was the home of the Holy Grail. I extended the line drawn in the other direction and I noticed that it went directly through somewhere called Saint Cross on the Isle of Wight. I put Saint Cross, Isle of Wight in to the internet search engine and couldn't believe my eyes. The small priory of the Holy Cross at the north end of the town of Newport, Isle of Wight, was an Alien priory, a cell of the Benedictine abbey of Tiron, founded in about 1120. Another Alien priory, a Benedictine Priory, just like Ellingham. Both Benedictine, both French, both perfectly aligned to Shaftesbury and Glastonbury!

I looked up Shaftesbury. It was the largest and most famous Benedictine monastery in England.

I extended the line on the greaseproof paper further, as far as my map would allow. It went through Llangennith and ended in Saint Davids, both in Wales.

Llangennith was the site of the Abbey of Cennydd, an Alien Benedictine Priory founded in the sixth century. The monks of Saint Taurin lived here. The Benedictines were in Wales in the 6th century? Surely this must have been one of the first Benedictine abbeys in

Britain. It was even older than Saint Davids, Saint Davids being one of the great historic shrines of Christendom. So now I had a line, along which lay six Benedictine abbeys, including some of the earliest Christian sites in the world. **(diag 1)** This could not be mere chance because they were so perfectly aligned. On this line also sat the modest church of Ellingham. But this was just a straight line, not a pentagram. I wanted to find a pentagram!

I went back to the map and tried drawing a line due north and south of Ellingham to see which places it went through. Once more I found an alignment with the sites of ancient Benedictine priories. Except for one. Temple Rockley was different. It was Knights Templar!

The only information I could find on Temple Rockley was that it was owned by the Knights Templars from the mid-twelfth century until 1308. But what about before 1308? My guess is that it was formerly home to the Benedictines. It could not be coincidence that their church was perfectly and accurately aligned with the Benedictine abbeys, priories and cells.

I carried on drawing my line due north and eventually the line went through the tiny island of Lindisfarne, Holy Island. Along with Glastonbury, this was the birthplace of Christianity in Britain. So in a way it didn't matter which was the actual birthplace as they were both featured on my line out of Ellingham. What was really strange was the fact that the line also went through the small towns in Northumberland and Durham where my parents were born, and the line went straight through my own home in Bournemouth! This was becoming curious. **(diag 2)**

My kitchen table was piled high with maps. Every time I needed to eat they had to be cleared away. This research wasn't easy in my current situation. I took a piece of A4 paper and sketched my findings to date. I had two lines, one going due north and south and one vaguely north west to south east. They crossed at Ellingham.

Southbourne

Bournemouth

Amesbury (Amblesberie)

Wooton Wawen

Lindisfarne

What did they all have in common?

All the names had eleven letters.

(Amesbury has eight letters but was known as Amblesberie in the old days: 11 letters).

The line going the other way started on the Isle of Wight and went through Ellingham, Shaftesbury, Glastonbury, Llangennith and Saint Davids.

Isle of Wight

Shaftesbury

Glastonbury

Llangennith

Saint Davids

What did they all have in common?

Eleven letters.

Benedictine.

Eleven letters.

Jesus Christ.

Eleven letters.

Now I had two lines and lots of places with eleven letters that had a common link with the Benedictines and the Knights Templars. But I couldn't see a pentagram. I started playing around with my protractor looking for any kind of mathematical shapes. If I took Glastonbury and Ellingham as two points on a triangle, they met at Clatford. The distance from Glastonbury to the Benedictine cell of Clatford was the same as the distance from Glastonbury to Ellingham, so I now had my first geometric shape, a triangle. I picked up a small notebook and drew a triangle, writing the place name at each point; Ellingham, Clatford and Glastonbury. Studying the map once more I found another one. Again, a triangle between Ellingham, Poling and Wallingford. Wallingford had a Benedictine priory and was also home to two hospitals in the thirteenth century, one dedicated to Mary Magdalene and the other to John the Baptist. Two key players in the Da Vinci mystery.

The Knights Hospitallers were at Poling, where it was said that ghosts of monks and Knights could be heard singing Gregorian Chants.

That reminded me of Karalyn hearing the monks chanting in the cellar in her home in Ugijar, opposite the convent. And I too had heard them.

There was an illustration of the seal of Wallingford alongside the above quote. A seated figure holding a book or a tablet in one hand and the other hand is making a gesture, the same gesture that John the Baptist makes in the painting by Da Vinci, which also features in The Last Supper. The pointing finger.

And so it went on. I discovered more and more equilateral triangles coming out of Ellingham. Soon the kitchen bench was covered with pieces of paper on which I had drawn all the triangles I had discovered. It was beginning to look like a complex geometric grid. **(diag 3)** My mapping so far had linked Ellingham directly with Lindisfarne and Glastonbury and also to Saint Davids. It had direct links with the most ancient and powerful sites of early Christianity. But I hadn't yet found a pentagram.

A thought came to me from nowhere. All I needed to do was to draw a circle and find five places equally spaced on the circumference of the circle. I had an intuitive feeling that my cousin John was linked to this whole scenario so I made the circle just big enough to encompass his local town, Chichester. My intuition was right. I had my perfect pentagram. **(diag 4)** At this time in my life it was as if my intuition was much stronger than it ever had been. I recalled reading about intuition in the Yoga Sutras, the teachings of Yoga. I looked up the quote I had remembered reading.

'All things can be known in the vivid light of the intuition.' *Yoga Sutras. Book 3 Sutra 33.*

3 and 33. I think I had expected it to be 1. 11.

Now I had satisfied my desire for finding a pentagram, I needed to know if Ellingham was linked to Ugijar. I would have to go and buy a map of Europe tomorrow. I had had enough of staring at maps for now. Stacking all my paperwork and books on the kitchen work surface, I began to cook dinner. As I started to peel the potatoes the phone rang. It was my friend Catherine, the friend who had strongly encouraged me to get in touch with Sabberan.

"I just thought I'd connect with you to see what's going on with you at the moment. Is everything ok?"

"Yes." I replied. "I'm writing a book about the convent at the moment. I'm writing about it because it's been such an odd series of events, especially around the number 11. I'm a bit stuck though because I really don't understand this number and what it means."

"The 11:11?" asked Catherine.

"Yes."

"That's all about the ascension process. It's all linked to 2012 when we are supposed to be experiencing the shifting of the earth poles," she explained.

"What? The end of the world?"

"No, but a big change."

"What do you think is going to happen? Do you think the earth is going to tilt on its axis that year?"

I knew that the earth was already tilted at 23 degrees because of my former mind-boggling experiences with coincidences concerning the number 23.

"It has been prophesised by many mystics and seers. Especially the ancient Mayan civilization. They were very precise with the date, winter solstice 2012. So if I were you I'd celebrate Christmas early that year!" she joked.

"No. Seriously. Do you think the earth will shift or get hit by a huge comet and we'll all get drowned?"

"Not necessarily. If enough people wake up then I don't think it will have to be that drastic. It depends on us really. We are each able to hold light and if enough of us are holding enough light, then the transition period will be much smoother."

"But why should I have experienced the 11:11 just around certain places. Like the old church in Ellingham and all that 11:11 around the convent in Ugijar?"

"Because these places are vortexes."

"Is that the same as portals?"

"Yes, you could call them portals. These are the places where the light is going to anchor. If any of these portals are blocked then it's going to affect the energy flow to other places. Just like in acupuncture. If you have a block in one of your acupuncture points it affects the flow of energy along the meridians of the body and you can get ill."

Catherine was saying exactly what Sabberan had said.

"Thanks Catherine. That makes it much clearer."

It all sounded a bit 'new age' to me. But I did take note of what she had said because of the 11:11 happening in my everyday life. Not as imagination but as fact.

I went back to my bowl of potatoes. And then a vision came to me as I looked down at the perfectly round potato I was peeling. It was much stronger and clearer vision than the one I had experienced before I bought the convent. The Earth, suspended in space, surrounded by light. But it was not complete, unbroken light. It was a complicated geometric design of light and wherever the lines on this design crossed at major junctions, it 'clicked' into place on the earth. It lined up perfectly. This vast geometric grid of light, aligned to the earth and once it was perfectly aligned, it found a perfect counterpart on the Earth itself at places that were ready and waiting to accept the light. Places that had been waiting for thousands of years. Places like Glastonbury, Saint Davids, Ellingham and Ugijar. Somehow those early Christians had knowledge of the grid. They knew where the portals were and so they chose those places to build their sacred churches. The proof was there in the siting of the early churches. They had been getting ready for 2012.

Ugijar, a place on the grid where lots of lines crossed, had been a place of murder and torture. So much darkness had accumulated at the convent that the grid was clogged, and so it had to be cleared. Through following the 11:11 signs I had been given, I had followed a higher power within myself rather than making a decision based on investment potential and suitability for a yoga center. I hadn't really wanted to spend all my money on this dilapidated, spooky place that gave me the creeps. But something beyond the little 'me' obviously wanted me to.

Winter Solstice 2012. What could be happening on that day? I decided to draw up a horoscope to see if there were any remarkable planetary line ups on that day. So I looked in my ephemeris to check the time of the solstice in that particular year because, like the signs of the zodiac, the day that the sun moves into a different sign varies from year to year. People who are born around the day of the change over are said to be born 'on the cusp'. For example somebody born on the twentieth of March could be either a Pisces or an Aries, depending on the year in which they were born. The winter solstice is the day that the sun moves into Capricorn. It was normally the 21st of December but it can be the 22nd. I drew the chart for the 21st and then started adjusting it until the sun was at zero degrees of Capricorn. I started at midday and went back one minute at a time until I had the very moment of the solstice. I kept on pressing the 'back' button, going back until I saw the symbol for 0 Capricorn appear. When I eventually saw the zero I froze the chart for that moment. I really couldn't believe the time that it was happening. The precise time of the solstice, the time of the entry of the sun into Capricorn in 2012 was exactly 11.11am.

I thought I had got to the point where I couldn't be startled by huge coincidences but I obviously hadn't because I just could not take in this information. I just didn't believe my eyes. Maybe I had made a mistake with my calculations? Maybe the computer was playing games with me? Once again reason tried to get me out of this huge synchronicity. I needed to double-check the calculations so I went back onto the internet and looked up the solstice list provided by NASA. They were bound to have the correct data. And there it was. I was not mistaken. There it was in black and white, officially correct, confirmed by NASA, 11.11am.

Date and Time of Solstice and Equinox

year	Equinox Mar day	time	Solstice June day	time	Equinox Sept day	time	Solstice Dec day	time
2002	20	19:16	21	13:24	23	04:55	22	01:14
2003	21	01:00	21	19:10	23	10:47	22	07:04
2004	20	06:49	21	00:57	22	16:30	21	12:42
2005	20	12:33	21	06:46	22	22:23	21	18:35
2006	20	18:26	21	12:26	23	04:03	22	00:22
2007	21	00:07	21	18:06	23	09:51	22	06:08
2008	20	05:48	20	23:59	22	15:44	21	12:04
2009	20	11:44	21	05:45	22	21:18	21	17:47
2010	20	17:32	21	11:28	23	03:09	21	23:38
2011	20	23:21	21	17:16	23	09:04	22	05:30
2012	20	05:14	20	23:09	22	14:49	21	11:11
2013	20	11:02	21	05:04	22	20:44	21	17:11
2014	20	16:57	21	10:51	23	02:29	21	23:03

This was a defining moment for me. I now knew without a shadow of a doubt that I was dealing with something big. This was a major piece of the puzzle falling perfectly into place.

The grid of light was made up of straight geometric lines. These small spiritual communities and churches were located at exactly the right location to make up the geometrical shapes required for the grid to anchor. The lines were straight, just like the number one. 1. 11. 111. 1111. And the lines were connected to each other by specific angles.

So the number one, eleven, one hundred and eleven and eleven /eleven appearing in everyday life, beyond chance, was the grid of light showing itself. The fact that they were coming in thick and fast showed that the light was drawing near.

My mind was reeling and I was out of milk so I walked down the road to my local shop to buy some milk and to get some fresh air. The milk was £1.11p. It struck me as a strange price for milk. I grabbed a couple of other things and paid. My change was 22p, twice 11. Was the local One Stop 24-hour convenience shop a portal? Maybe I was a walking portal. Or was I going mad? It was both disturbing and exciting the way that 11:11 kept appearing but it was a fine line between sanity and insanity. It was only faith that I was on to something big that was keeping me sane.

CHAPTER TWENTY ONE

I was still devouring everything and anything I could on the Da Vinci code, to see if there were any more clues for me regarding the Knights Templars which might throw some light on the convent. On May 13th there was a television program setting out to investigate the claims of the books *Holy Blood, Holy Grail* and *The Da Vinci Code*. It was the usual stuff, the history of the Cathars and the Priory of Sion and the priest in Rennes Le Chateau who had suddenly become rich. Then there was the obligatory visit to Rosslyn Chapel near Edinburgh which I had visited the year before.

The program did confirm that the Templars had invented international banking and that in 1311 the Pope had dissolved the Templar Order. So the information that Kevyn had given me was correct.

There was a reference to the Grail possibly being Jesus Christ's head that reminded me of the rumors that the Templars had worshipped the head of John the Baptist. The reference to John the Baptist had been Chapter 11, verse 11 of the Gospel of Matthew. Using 11:11 as a sign, then John the Baptist must have been involved in this plot somewhere.

The trail eventually led the investigating team of journalists to the controversial painting by Da Vinci. They stood in front of Leonardo's The Last Supper in the Dominican Convent of Santa Maria delle Grazie in Milan, Italy. The entire camera crew and the interviewer were discussing the figure seated to Jesus's right and were unanimous in their verdict that it was indeed a woman sitting at the right hand of Jesus. But they were being told by the historian who they were interviewing that it was not a woman, it was John. It was a bit like looking at a tree and somebody saying, "That's not a tree, that's a flower."

They were discussing the V shape in the middle of the painting and whether or not that was representative of a vessel or a letter M. It was undeniable that right in the center of the painting, Jesus and Mary were seated apart in such a way that they formed a distinct V shape. The letter V. What could that stand for? Could it be V for Vinci? I took note of the fact that it was the twenty second letter of the alphabet, twice 11. It's not just the 11 I look out for these days. I take note of any repeated numerals.

There were 13 people in the painting. Nothing special about that. But if it was Mary Magdalene on Jesus's right and Mary and Jesus were a couple, how many guests were at the dinner?

11.

"And there's nothing behind Mary/John and Jesus. It's not as if there is anything relevant in the background," stated the investigating journalist.

I examined the background, just as they were doing. It hit me smack between the eyes. A huge great number eleven. Right in the center, right behind Jesus. The two pillars made a number eleven, just like the twin towers in New York made a number eleven on the skyline. Just like the twin towers in New York made the number 11 out of concrete and glass, the pillars made two ones out of stone and plaster. Jesus was sitting right between these two pillars, sitting in the middle of a number 11. How come I had never spotted that before? Now I could see it, it just seemed so obvious. Was I going crazy? Was I seeing 11's where 11's didn't exist? Was this simply my over active imagination? Was it only obvious to me because I was so tuned in to the number 11 now?

"And nowhere else in the background of the painting is there any symbolism," continued the historian.

I counted the large rectangles in the background of the painting, four on the right, four on the left. What were they? I thought maybe they were wall hangings or rectangular panels. Then right behind Jesus and Mary were three large rectangular openings. So that makes eleven large rectangles in total. Four plus four plus three. Eleven. I re-counted them. Yes, I was not imagining it. There were eleven large rectangles. So right there in the painting of the last Supper was the 11:11. Not just once, but twice. The 11 rectangles were indisputable, unlike the figure on Jesus's right hand.

If I had managed to miss a huge number 11 in the very center of the painting to this day, what else had I missed?

Hands were such a strong feature of this painting it was as if Da Vinci was shouting at me to look at the hands. I counted as carefully as I could and it certainly looked as if 11 hands were visible to either side of Jesus. I would have to get a copy of the Last Supper and check that carefully.

He was telling us so clearly about the 11:11. I was getting worried. Worried and excited at the same time. Why should Da Vinci be putting elevens in this painting? I kept looking at the hands. I knew the message would reveal itself to me if I looked for long enough. The two hands of Jesus lay one below each of the two pillars that made up the figure 11 in the center of the painting, as if he is holding up this number, saying, 'Look at me. I am in the center of the painting and what are my hands doing? Look at where they are. One hand under each numeral.' His hands were not pointing at anybody or making a gesture. They were simply laid in perfect alignment with the two pillars. One hand under each of the two pillars.

One of the disciples was holding up one finger, a signal which appears in a few of Da Vincis paintings. The pointed finger. What did a finger represent? This was such a strong gesture, I knew it must be a huge clue. I racked my brains. What was he saying with this finger? What could a finger represent? Was there another word for a finger? Yes. The other word for a finger was a digit. A digit was also the word used for any of the numbers from one to nine. Did this mean that the answer to the puzzle of Da Vinci's pointing digit is a number? The pointing finger was Da Vinci telling us about a number from one to nine. Think digit! And the fact that he was using only the index finger made me realise that he was indicating the numeral 1. How would one use a hand gesture to indicate the number 11? Thinking about it, I realized you couldn't use only two hands to indicate 11 because we only have ten fingers. We could only indicate up to ten. But we could indicate number one. And how would we do that? Exactly as DaVinci has shown us on his paintings. We would raise up our index finger!

I checked this out on a few friends. Every person I asked, child, old person, educated, uneducated, male, female, English, foreign, gave exactly the same response. They all showed me the index finger in exactly the manner painted by Leonardo Da Vinci.

The Da Vinci finger gesture is 1. 11. 111. 1111.

What's more, the upwards pointing finger in *The Last Supper* was in front of the pillar which represented one of the two number ones in what I believed to represent the number 11. Out of the 29ft (2+9=11) or so available on the painting, Da Vinci had chosen this place for that finger.

To doubly make sure that he got his message regarding the 11:11 across, he had painted 11 fingers in this column/pillar. The painting is 30 feet wide and within a column of the painting less than one foot wide lie this interesting group of hands. How do you indicate five with your fingers? By opening the palm and displaying all the fingers. Once more I asked my bemused friends and family to show me how they would indicate five with their hands. They all, without exception, open one hand with the fingers apart. Nobody uses two fingers of one hand and three of another, or four of one hand and one on the other.

"Indicate ten please," I asked. They all displayed two open hands.

In the narrow section of the painting with the pointing finger Da Vinci had displayed two open palms and one pointing finger. Total=11. This cannot be coincidental.

The section of the painting with the dagger is also interesting. Dagger. What did this represent? Stabbing? Cutting? Was there another word for a dagger? Blade? I looked in my Collins Concise

English dictionary. The word 'blade' was found on page 111 of my dictionary. I laughed! But there were no meanings that I could immediately link to the 11:11. Maybe it had been put there as a symbol of betrayal, indicating that we had been betrayed by having the truth hidden from us?

Once again in the section of the painting with the dagger we have two open palms, totaling the number ten, and by putting the dagger in this part of the painting, the long blade could have been used to represent the eleventh digit.

I carefully counted the number of hands that could be seen on the painting, using a digital copy of the Last Supper. This was not an easy task but I was certain that there were indeed eleven visible hands to the right of Jesus and eleven to the left. Da Vinci must surely have known about the 11:11. Had he experienced the amazing coincidences around this number just like I had? Did he know about the grid of light too? Was there anything to indicate this? Having shown us the 11:11, how could he show the grid?

The ceiling of the Last Supper is a grid, not just a plain ceiling, possibly suggesting the grid of light. The tablecloth has been folded and opened out, the creases leaving a grid like imprint on the cloth. A huge expanse of tablecloth would have been a perfect opportunity for Da Vinci to demonstrate his skill at painting draped cloth, but instead he has chosen a neat, newly unfolded cloth. By doing this I believe that he had repeated the message of the grid.

Now I had started linking number to this painting I could not stop. The more I stared at *The Last Supper*, the more was revealed. The next thing that leaped out at me was the composition of the figures. The figures in the painting were not evenly spaced nor were they randomly spaced. They were in distinct and separate groups, so much so that it was quite clear that they had been deliberately formed into groups of 3 3 1 3 and 3. Once I realized this, it was blindingly obvious. The grouping of the figures was very distinct and I was certain that there must have been a numeric message here.

33.1.33, triple 11 each side of a single numeral. Why? What was the relevance of the 33? It was a double digit, just like the 11, but what was the message? It had appeared before in the yoga sutra, concerning intuition. Chapter 3, Sutra 33. Try as I might I couldn't solve this one. I would have to leave that for another day.

There were just too many things here to ignore. It was as if now I could see the code, I was in on the secret and Da Vinci was drumming it home. I was now in no doubt that he must have known about 2012.

I needed to look more closely at Da Vinci's work but the local libraries had very few books about him. So I rang a friend who, as an art lecturer, had a comprehensive art library. I rang him at home and as his answer phone message ended I prepared to leave a message. He was normally in his studio painting during the day. But he picked up the phone and answered in person. I must have caught him during a coffee break.

"Hi Miles. I just wondered if you had any books about Leonardo Da Vinci that I could borrow."

There was a silence whilst he took in what I had just said.

"I have a book about Da Vinci right here on the shelf. I've just bought it!"

From this book I learned that Da Vinci was known as Leonardo Da Vinci because he was born in Vinci (V=22nd letter of the alphabet).

He was born on 15.4.1452. 1+5+4+1+4+5+2=22.

The Last Supper was 29ft wide (2+9=11)

A different source stated it is 28ft 10ins. Still it adds up to 11. (2+8+1=11).

Da Vinci was known for his use of the golden mean in his paintings. This is also known as Divine Proportion. It was based on the Fibonnacci series of numbers which starts with 0. 1. 1. 2. 3. 5. 8. (The first number is added to the second, the second to the third, the third to the fourth and so on.)

This series of numbers creates a spiral which can be found everywhere in nature, from DNA to the spiral of a seashell. The rooms in the convent were rectangular. It crossed my mind that they might have been constructed according to the golden mean. As I went in search of the architects plans of the convent, for once I was thankful for the bureaucracy of Ugijar town hall, who had insisted on these plans being drawn. At the time this was just an unwanted expense and bother, but now I was delighted that the architect had been called in. Obviously a building as old as the convent had been changed around a lot over the centuries but the original earth walls still remained. Knocking down a one meter thick earth wall was not an easy task. So I only looked at the proportions of the rooms with earth walls, not the more recently divided ones.

The room where I found the feather was 960cm x 600cm according to the plans. They have been drawn on a scale of 1:100. Using the calculator on my mobile phone I put in 960 divided by 600. The answer was 1.6.

1.61803 is the golden mean. I was right! It had been built to the golden mean, far too accurately to be mere chance.

I measured the room I was intending to use as a yoga studio. 1100x660.

Answer 1.6. This confirmed it.

These two downstairs back rooms were rectangular. The rooms at the front of the convent were irregular because the front of the convent had been built at an angle, so each of the two front rooms have two angles of 90 degrees, one of 105 degrees and one of 75 degrees. I had never attached any significance to this fact before other than thinking it a bit unusual. With so much land available, why build at a strange angle? Now I think that this might have been intentional. The convent is on a street called Las Meridas, which runs due north and south. Meridas is a very similar word to Meridian and I guessed that maybe the convent had been lined up in a certain direction. Maybe it had been lined up to the north and south poles?

The fact that this old convent had been home to the Knights Templars but was not round like some of the old Templar churches had puzzled me. Now that I could see that it had been built using the golden mean I was delighted. This confirmed that the convent had been built by people with the knowledge of sacred geometry. **(diag 5)**

CHAPTER TWENTY TWO

I was still waiting to hear from Sabberan. He was in a caravan somewhere writing a book so he wasn't too easy to get hold of. I looked up his website Iona-Light.co.uk to get hold of his phone number. Where was Iona? Iona was way up in the north, the Inner Hebrides. In 563AD Saint Columba had established a monastery here, from which Celtic Christianity had spread to Scotland and Europe. The original wooden buildings were no longer there, but the present building dated from around 1200 when it was in the hands of the Benedictines.

This was not a surprise. Now I was expecting this connection between the Benedictines and these ancient sacred sites. But I still had not found the link between Ellingham and Ugijar. So I opened my newly acquired map of Europe out on the dining room table and, because my ruler wasn't long enough, I took a long piece of wood. I lined up Lindisfarne with Ugijar. Did it go through Ellingham?

No.

I lined up Iona with Ugijar. Does it go through Ellingham?

No.

I tried the same for Iona and Saint Davids in Wales.

No luck.

There must be a connection. But what? What connected Ellingham to Ugijar? Maybe it was simply that all the places on the grid were connected to each other because they were connected via the grid. This was why Sabberan had had to clear sites as far away as Israel and Egypt when he worked on unblocking the energy at the convent. But in my heart I knew there must be something more, something I had not yet spotted. It was just a matter of not giving up until I found it.

I had drawn a straight line on the map of Europe, between Ugijar and Ellingham. I realized that these were both tiny and seemingly insignificant places on the map. Ellingham had less than a hundred residents, Ugijar less than three thousand. Insignificant in terms of their size, that is. Neither of them were marked on the map, despite the fact that I had bought the largest scale sheet map of Europe available in the most comprehensive bookshop in town. So I calculated their position as accurately as possible and marked them with a dot.

Now what? Am I going to be looking for a pentagram? Or a six sided star? Or an equilateral triangle? My eyes scanned the bookcase, looking for any books I might have that show geometric shapes. I needed inspiration. *The City of Revelation* by John Mitchell caught my eye. It was an old book, printed in 1973, but as I flicked through it I could see that there were some geometric drawings. Rather too complicated ones for me. So I turned to page 111, reasoning that if this book had a message, that's the page it would be on. There was no drawing on this page but there was something far more interesting. THE MAGIC SQUARE OF THE SUN. I had never heard of this. It was a square containing the numbers 1 through to 36. They were arranged in such a way that whenever one added up a column it added up to 111. Wow! Was it coincidence that this magic square of 111 appears on page 111? Was it just in this particular edition of the book that this synchronicity occurred? Whatever the case, this was a revelation to me. The 111 being recognized in a mathematical square.

As I sat pondering the map with the line drawn between Ellingham and Ugijar, I noticed the Da Vinci book that I had borrowed from my friend Miles was lying open at the page of *The Last Supper*. What else did Da Vinci have to say to me?

My eye fell on the V near the center of the painting between Jesus and Mary Magdalene. Jesus and Mary Magdalene were leaning away from each other at quite a sharp angle. Taking my protractor I lined it up, using the end of their noses as the mid line and I measured the gap: 90 degrees. Okay. Maybe that was a clue. I measured the angle between their bodies. Again it was 90 degrees. It was definitely a clue.

So I marked the point midway between Ellingham and Ugijar and drew a line across at 90 degrees. It went straight through the Vatican! Right through the very heart of the Roman Catholic church.

The Vatican is another letter V too (22). Is that what that gap between Mary and Jesus was? Was it a V? Only the V did not stand for a vessel but for the Vatican.

Joining the Vatican to Ellingham and Ugijar created a triangle with two sides of equal length and one slightly longer. When I measured the angles of this triangle I noticed that two of them were 57 degrees and the vertex angle which came out of the Vatican was 66 degrees, giving 33 degrees either side of the dissecting line. I made the connection immediately. 33 features in Da Vinici's Last Supper, two groups of three either side of Jesus (33 1 33). The convent and Ellingham were giving me the same message as Da Vinci. **(diag 6)**

This was curious. Rome and the Vatican were now involved in my 11:11 mystery. So was the number 33. Twice 33 was 66, the angle of my isosceles triangle linking Ellingham, Ugijar and The Vatican. I reminded myself that although the Vatican was now the center of the Roman Catholic Church, it was built on the site of a much older church. This site was allegedly where Simon was crucified. I also knew that the number 33 featured strongly in the Masonic movement, being the highest grade attainable. Was this a clue that might link the Templars to the masons?

I vaguely remembered reading that Da Vinci had studied in Rome so once more I searched the internet for details about Da Vinci's life. He had indeed spent time in Rome. He had joined Bramante, Gabriel, and Michelangelo in Rome to work for Pope Leo X. These four great artists had worked on designs and construction of the new Church of St Peter. Some of them had also worked on other new or enlarged buildings and rooms in the Vatican. Several French kings admired Leonardo's work and invited him to live in France. Da Vinci finally accepted Francis I's invitation in 1516, and settled in the small castle of Cloux, near Amboise. He lived there in a princely fashion until he died, on May 2, 1519.

He had been involved in the design of Saint Peters and might well have worked on the Vatican! There he was, right in the heart of Rome.

All this research, sitting at the computer and leaning over maps, was taking its toll on my back. I had been working non-stop for hours, with rain lashing against the windows. The good thing about English rain was that it did vary in its intensity (unlike the rain in the Alpujarras) so as soon as there was a gap in the weather I jumped on my bike and headed down to the bottom of the road to see the sea. It was a windy day and the cool sea air was blowing hard, perfect for clearing my head. As I left the road and rode up onto the grass I saw a familiar figure, my old friend Stewart.

"Hey, long time no see, Hilary."

"Stewart!" I exclaimed, giving him a hug. "How are you?"

"I'm well. I haven't seen you in ages. What have you been up to?"

" I'm in the middle of writing a book. In fact I've only come out to clear my head."

"What's it about? Not the Bible code is it?"

"The Bible Code?"

"Yes, last time I saw you – it must have been a couple of years ago – you were telling me about the Bible code."

"Yes, I remember reading that book."

"You know they de-bunked that theory don't you? They used the same idea but taking a novel rather than the Bible and found exactly the same sort of messages. It was all a hoax."

"Well they can't de-bunk what I'm writing about because most of it can be proved," I retorted.

That was true. There were certain indisputable facts.

I had the email sent at 11.11 from Katarina.

77,000GBP was the equivalent of 11110euros in 2004.

Matthew 11 11 mentions John the Baptist.

11 11 is Armistice day.

All the figures around 9/11 and the twin towers can be checked and proved.

The estate agent was born on 11 Nov.

Winter Solstice 2012 is at 11.11am exactly.

$21.12.2012 = 2+1+1+2+2+1+2 = 11$

The 11th letter K ; Katarina, Karalyn, Kevyn

The 22nd letter V for the Vatican.

The symbols of 11's in The Last Supper.

There was more. The list was long.

"So what's your book about?"

"The Da Vinci Code. I think I've cracked it. I've discovered a message in numbers that Da Vinci wanted to tell us."

His look said it all, the slightly amused yet affectionate expression. Almost a smirk.

"But I have. I can prove it. Unlike a lot of Dan Brown's stuff, which is subjective, mine is factual. Mine is to do with numbers and angles, coincidences that can be proved."

"Oh yes. What do you mean? Da Vinci painted by numbers!"

"Actually he did. For a start he painted using the golden mean, which was based on a mathematical formula. All you have to do is open any book on the composition of T*he Last Supper* and the golden mean features time and time again. That's not a guess. It's a measurable fact."

"What does that prove?"

"Have you not heard of sacred geometry? Da Vinci was not just a painter. In fact if you count up all his paintings you will realize that he produced very few. He was an all-rounder, an inventor, architect, sculptor, engineer and mathematician. It proves he had knowledge of this mathematical formula for a start. I think he was using his art to get his message across. He was combining art with mathematics."

"And what is his message?"

"The ultimate message in that painting is that he knew about the ending of the Mayan calendar. The Mayan calendar ends on winter solstice in 2012."

"It had to end sometime."

"Yes I agree. And if it suddenly ended on July 13th or August 2nd or some other inconsequential date then I wouldn't be so impressed. The fact that it ends on the solstice indicates that the Mayans knew something."

"There's a winter solstice every year. What's so special about 2012?"

"Do you actually know what the winter solstice is?"

"Yes, it's the 21st December, the shortest day of the year."

"To be more precise it is the day that the sun moves into Capricorn, so it doesn't have to be the 21st. It can actually be the 20th or the 22nd. Just like the signs of the zodiac the exact date varies year to year."

"And you reckon Da Vinci knew this?"

"I do. And he's put that symbolism in *The Last Supper*. Take a look at that painting. A huge number 11 just behind Christ, 11 huge rectangles in the background and 11 guests of Jesus and Mary. Either side of Christ there are 11 hands that can be seen, even though there are six people to each side of him. In the second column of what I believe to be representing the number eleven there are eleven fingers, including that pointing finger. Another group of 11 fingers in the bit where there is a knife. And the tablecloth even bears creases in the form of a grid, which I think is representative of the grid of light. He's trying to get us to see a grid. The ceiling's a grid too. That's why he has put two grids in the painting. He couldn't have done much more, other than having one of the figures holding up a placard saying 'eleven eleven'."

"So why has he got an obsession with the number 11?"asked Stewart. "The solstice isn't on the 11th. And you're not talking about 2011, you're talking about 2012. What is so relevant about the number

11? Is it a code?"

"The winter solstice in 2012 will take place at 11.11am. And it is a code. It's a code that appears in your everyday life where you can see it."

"I thought there were thirteen people in that painting. Jesus and the twelve disciples."

"Yes there are thirteen people in total, but that's more symbolism. It brings us back to the Mayan calendar. We have periods of time called years and centuries and so on. The Mayans have periods of time called Baktuns. Thirteen baktuns from the start of the calendar to the end brings us exactly to winter solstice 2012. It's the end of a major cycle. Hence the thirteen figures in the painting, each one representing a baktun."

Stewart looked thoughtful.

"You haven't answered my question. Why the 11? Why is the code not 12 if the big day is going to happen in 2012?" he asked.

"Add up 21 12 2012 and it comes to 11. The solstice will take place at 11.11 in the morning. 11 is a master number in numerology," I explained, impatiently. "If you add up the numbers in your date of birth you can find out what life path you are on, which indicates the lessons you have come to learn in this particular life. When were you born?"

"The 18th October 1964."

"Okay. So add 1 to 8, which is 9. Then 1 to 0, which is 1. 1+9+6+4 equals 20. 2 plus 0 is 2. Add the 9 to the 1 to the 2 which gives 12. 1 plus 2 equals 3. So your life path is 3."

"What does that mean?"

"The 3 life path is about expressing the joy of living yet not wasting energy."

"What's yours? Let me guess. It's the 11!"

"No. I'm on the 5 path which is all about freedom. I'm seeking the ultimate freedom, which is freedom from the wheel of rebirth.

Numbers are fascinating. After all, it was numbers that set me on this journey. I had huge coincidences around the number 11 at an old church near Ringwood. Ellingham church. Do you know it?"

"No."

"Not many people do. It's a small church at the end of a dead end road, just off the Ringwood to Salisbury road. I was with Anthony, my ex-boyfriend. It was Armistice day, 11/11. Everywhere we looked that day we were surrounded by the number 11."

"Can you prove that?"

"I can prove that Armistice day is the eleventh of November. Everybody knows that, the 11/11 day that we acknowledge each year. Normally hundreds of thousands of people stop what they're doing and stand in silence. On the 11th of the 11th at 11 o'clock. There's no other day or time that we do that, is there?"

"No, you're right," he conceded. "We don't even have anything like that on Christmas Day or at Easter."

"So I find it really odd that the number 11 is so strongly associated with Armistice Day. It's not just me experiencing this 11:11 phenomena. It's happening to people all over the world and I think it's a sign that the world as we know it is about to change. But there's more, Stewart. If I draw a line between the convent and Ugijar, find the mid-point and then take a line out at 90 degrees, guess where it goes through."

"Mmmm. Which direction?"

"East."

"Florence?"

"No. Think!"

Stewart puckered his forehead, racking his brains.

"Majorca?"

"No. The Vatican."

Stewart's eyebrows raised momentarily.

"I have discovered an isosceles triangle between three places. And

I'm not talking about any three places. I'm talking about two places that had huge coincidences around the number eleven and the third one is the center of the Roman Catholic church. I was trying to find out how these two places were linked to each other and I think the link with the Vatican is pretty amazing."

Why should there be this link with the Vatican?

Da Vinci had been invited to Milan by Ludovico Sforza. Sforza was known as *il moro*, meaning the Moor or Moroccan because of his unusually dark complexion. Was he in fact a Moor? I find this fact particularly interesting because of the strong Moorish connection to Ugijar. The Moors had lived in Ugijar since the eighth century and were the guardians of a lot of ancient wisdom.

Da Vinci remained in Milan for almost 20 years and it was during this period that he painted *The Virgin on the Rocks* and *The Last Supper*. It was after this time with the Moor that he painted *Virgin and Child with Saint Anne* and the portrait of John the Baptist with the pointing finger. His final statement. His last message. Clear and simple. John the Baptist and the numeral 1.

It is also interesting to note that John the Baptist has not got his thumb tucked back when he points his finger. Is Da Vinci suggesting the shadow of a second number one, the 11?

CHAPTER TWENTY THREE

The last known work of Da Vinci was the painting of John the Baptist This was his DaVinci's last, John the Baptist with a pointing finger. There was no doubt in my mind that Da Vinci was trying to tell us something about John the Baptist. What was it that he knew and that he wanted us to know? Was the message of Da Vinci's *Madonna of the yarn winder* that we had been spun a yarn and that John the Baptist was the true prophet? I felt guilty just thinking that thought because my conditioning had been so strong. Brought up as a Methodist by the daughter of a lay preacher, I had attended church from the moment I was born and I was Christened in the 11th week of my life. Now for the first time in my life it crossed my mind that maybe I was the victim of a huge conspiracy.

I opened my Bible, presented to me on my Christening day, May 1st by my godmother Joy Couzens, sister of my cousin John who had died after loaning me the money to buy the convent.

It opened on Luke Chapter 11. My eyes alighted on verse 1. *'And it came to pass that as he was praying in a certain place, when he ceased, one of his disciples said unto him, Lord, teach us to pray, as John also taught his disciples.'* (Luke11.1)

111 being linked with John the Baptist again. And I had opened it on this page. What were the chances of that? There were almost 900 pages in this particular Bible.

'Teach us to pray, as John taught his disciples.'

So John had disciples, followers whom he had taught to pray. Was Jesus a disciple of John? I already had the gospel of Matthew linked with John the Baptist 11.11.

'I tell you this; never has there appeared on earth a mother's son greater than John the Baptist, and yet the least in the Kingdom of Heaven is greater than he.'

This was Luke 11.1. So I turned to Mark. Mark 1.1 *'John the Baptist prepares the way.'*

Wow!

1. The beginning of the gospel about Jesus Christ, the Son of God.[a] No mention of John the Baptist here, but what is in footnote (a)? Footnotes: Mark 1:1 *'Some manuscripts do not have the Son of God.'*

So was 'the Son of God' added at a later date, maybe in Nicea in 325AD when the text of the Bible was being decided on? If 'Son of God' was indeed added at a later date, Mark 1.1. would simply read *'The beginning of the Gospel about Jesus Christ'*. The footnote has drawn attention to the fact that maybe he was not the son of God.

By the time of his death John had already baptised thousands of people, including Jesus. Baptism is the washing away of sins. If Jesus had been the son of God then surely he would not have had any sins that needed washing away? In the Bible, which I now knew to be a selective book, it was claimed that John prepared the way for Jesus Christ. That was not necessarily true. Maybe John was the teacher of Jesus Christ. After all, it was John who had baptised Jesus, not the other way round.

The council of Nicea were highly selective when they were deciding what was going to be included in the Bible and their selections and translations would have had to fit their version of the truth. Many texts were simply not included, and certain books were completely discarded. So maybe huge chunks about John teaching Jesus had been left out.

The last of the four gospels I looked at was that of John. I took the New English Bible from the shelf and turned to John 1.1. *'When all things began, the Word already was'*.

Word had a capital letter. *'In the beginning was the Word and the Word was with God and the Word was God.'* This took us right back to the beginning of life itself.

It is fact that the content of the Bible was carefully selected. What we have in the Bible today is a selection of writings, some of which have been subject to dubious translations and editing. So we cannot trust the Bible to be the pure teaching of Jesus. We needed to look to Jesus's teacher. So if John the Baptist was the teacher of Jesus, what did he teach him?

My research on the internet for the teachings of John the Baptist quickly led me to the Mandaean people. Mandaeans revere John the Baptist as one of their greatest teachers. The Mandaean people who live mainly on the border of Iran and Iraq, rely heavily on the teachings of John the Baptist. Their religion is a proto-religion in which they descended from Adam who was the first to receive the religious instructions of the Mandaeans. Their last great teacher and healer was John the Baptist. The origins of both the people and of the religion are one of the continuing mysteries of Mandaean research.

John the Baptist is recognized by Christians and Muslims, but he is given a higher status in Mandaeism. They do not claim John the Baptist to be the founder of their religion, analogous to Jesus or Muhammad within Christianity and Islam. They maintain that he was merely one of their greatest teachers. According to their beliefs, Mandaeism was the original religion of Adam. That brings us back to John 1.1. *'In the beginning was the Word'*.

The Mandaeans believed that Jesus was a rebel who betrayed the secret Cabbalistic doctrines. John the Baptist was thought to be the truer teacher, skilled in magic and concerned with the healing of bodies and souls. This attitude is interpolated into some of their texts. I knew that the Cabbalists had lived in the Ugijar area because one of their churches still remained high up on the mountains, overlooking Ugijar, a tiny, deserted building, slowly crumbling to the ground. The church with the Star of David and the Christian cross on the roof that had baffled me when I first saw it.

Was this what Da Vinci knew, that John the Baptist was the truer teacher? His way of announcing his findings to the world was to hide clues in his paintings, knowing that when the time was right these clues would be unravelled and the truth would be exposed. That time was now, with the approach of 2012.

The primary sacred scripture of the Mandaean's is the Book of John the Baptizer. I looked up some more about their religious texts on www.mandaeans.org and discovered that in this religion men and women are equal and their prohibitions are:

1 Blasphemy

2 Murder

3 Adultery

4 Stealing

5 Telling lies

6 False testimony

7 Disloyalty and dishonesty

8 Lust

9 Magic and witchcraft

10 Circumcision

11 Alcoholic drinks

12 Usury

13 Crying over the dead

14 Eating dead animals, pregnant animals or animals attacked by other furious animals and blood

15 Divorce (save in some exceptional cases)

16 Suicide and abortion

17 Self-torturing, self-harming and body-hurting

The Mandaeans respect all heavenly religions in their society and the world at large. They live peacefully alongside Muslims and Christians as well as other religions. That reminds me of what Kevyn had told me about the time in history when various faiths lived alongside each other in peace in Ugijar. The Mandaeans have no history of violence or torture towards their fellow men. Although they have sacred scriptures, they do not have a prophet. Their prohibitions are the guidance by which they live.

So here is a group of people who have been heavily influenced by the teaching of John the Baptist and they are a peaceful people. No inquisitions. No holy wars. And no prophet. Just like yoga! In fact I was struck by the similarity of the Mandean teaching to the Eight Limbs of yoga which I had studied as part of my yoga teacher training course. These are a progressive series of steps or disciplines which purify the body and mind, ultimately leading the yogi to enlightenment. Enlightenment in this context means becoming one with God. The Eight Limbs are:

1 *Yamas* – Restraints aimed at destroying the lower nature, to be practiced in word, thought and deed. Non-violence, truthfulness, moderation in all things (also refers to celibacy), not stealing and not being possessive.

2 *Niyamas* – things to observe. Purity, contentment, discipline, study and surrender to Gods will. (Gods will being shown through signs such as numbers.)

3 *Asanas* – yoga postures, placing the physical body in certain poses.

4 *Pranayama* – control of the breath.

5 *Pratyahara* – withdrawal of the senses in order to still the mind.

6 *Dharana* – focusing the attention on one thing, concentration.

7 *Dhyana* – meditation where the mind encompasses an object and contemplates it with complete and unwavering attention.

8 *Samadhi* – a state of bliss beyond meditation, the super-conscious state. This is the deepest and highest state of consciousness where body and mind have been transcended and the yogi is one with the Self or God.

Yoga teaches us how to become enlightened. No prophet is required to reach enlightenment. Yoga teaches us how to transcend the physical body and the laws of the physical universe. It teaches us that, like Jesus or John the Baptist, or you or me or your next door neighbour, we are spiritual beings in a physical human body. But we're not just this body. We have a much finer counterpart of the human body known as the etheric or astral body. Yogis who have reached the state of *Samadhi* can appear or disappear at will. They can also 'bi-locate', appearing in different places at the same time. They can heal and read thoughts and other such 'miracles'. The yoga teaching is that this state of consciousness is available to anybody who is prepared to follow the eight limbs of yoga. It sounds simple in theory but it is not that easy in practise. I know, because that is how I try to live my life.

Following these principles I can see that we do not need priests or vicars to teach us about God. In fact, in many ways the church has stolen our Divinity from us by leading us away from the truth. The yoga teachings, Gnostic teachings like those of John the Baptist, teach us that we are Divine and they show us the way to realise our Divinity. Through yoga practises such as diet, postures, breath-work and meditation, we can reach such a high state of consciousness that the laws of the physical universe no longer confine us. We transcend the laws of the physical universe. This is demonstrated by yogis in India who can perform great feats, such as being buried alive for weeks. Yoga literature such as *Autobiography of a Yogi* tells of the great Yogi Babaji being able to appear and disappear at will.

John the Baptist was known to perform miracles. Had he followed the path of yoga? I believe he did. And maybe Da Vinci did too. I recall reading that Da Vinci was a vegetarian, which is part of the path of yoga. *'Leonardo da Vinci, the great artist, engineer and creator of the Mona Lisa, was such a fervent vegetarian that he would buy caged birds from poultry vendors and set them free.' Famous Vegetarians* by Professor Rynn Berry

Vegetarianism is not so unusual these days but in the times of Da Vinci it would have been much more unusual. I also believe he was celibate, rather than homosexual, having gained control of his sexual urges. In yoga we can raise our vibration by increasing the amount of prana we can store in the body and one of the ways of doing this is to abstain from sexual intercourse and use the sexual energy to raise our consciousness. Prana is pure energy, known as Chi in the Chinese system. If we all knew how to increase our prana we would all be vibrating at a much higher rate and the world would be a much safer and more peaceful place.

When I went to visit the famous Templar church at Rosslyn in Scotland I was astounded to see carvings of figures doing yoga postures. As a yoga teacher I recognised the postures, and I was really surprised to see them. They are not normally found in a church. I was sure they were put there as signs, as more clues. I heard that a musician had looked at the symbols on the columns at Rosslyn and had broken the code that linked them to musical notes. When he played the tune that was inscribed on these pillars it turned out to be the banned heretical hymn known as *Hymn to John the Baptist*.

Maybe Da Vinci was telling us to look at the Gnostic teachings of John the Baptist rather than take our instruction from the church. In that way we could have direct knowledge of God and claim our birthright, which is our own Divinity, rather than allow the church to feed us half truths that actually divert us from the path to that realization.

CHAPTER TWENTY FOUR

I had a dream last night. I was in the convent with Kevyn. There were Egyptian hieroglyphics on the walls. He had a pick-axe with him and started to dig. Within minutes he came across a large plastic parking cone, which had been put over the entrance of a dungeon to stop the earth falling into the space below. When he pulled out the cone there was a metal chest. The manuscripts!

Although it was Kevyn doing the digging in my dream this was unlikely to be the reality as I had lost his phone number and had no way of getting in touch with him. I racked my brain for somebody else who could dig instead of Rico Santos but there was nobody. I was not sure about Rico Santos. Could I trust him or not? I still hadn't heard from Sabberan so I didn't know if anything had been done about clearing his energy field. I wondered if my friend Dawn knew anybody strong and willing who could help me? I picked up the phone and start dialing her number.

"Hello?"

I had connected immediately, without the phone even ringing. Only that was not Dawn's voice.

"Hello. Who's that?"

"It's Sabberan."

How strange. He must have rung me and I picked up the phone at the instant he got through to me, before it had even started ringing.

"Sabberan! Great!"

"Is this a good time to ring?"

"Yes, perfect. I was just thinking about the convent at that very minute. I had a dream last night and it started me thinking about the dig."

"A dream? What about?"

"I dreamed that someone called Kevyn dug in the convent and

found a metal chest containing documents."

"You haven't started digging yet?" he asked.

"No. Because I wasn't sure about the state of Rico Santos's energy."

"You haven't done any clearing work on him?"

"No. I don't know how to. But I've had the okay to go ahead. His girlfriend Karalyn asked him if he was happy for us to work on his energy and he said yes."

At this point Sabberan tuned into Rico Santos's energy. Then he started releasing him from contracts of magic and religious organizations, using prayer and Divine intervention. Santos must have taken some pretty heavy vows in the past. After about ten minutes of prayers I could actually feel the energy change.

"It'll be safe to go ahead now," said Sabberan. "But just check it feels all right with you."

It did. All the feelings of distrust and disquiet had gone and it felt fine. At last. I couldn't wait to give Rico Santos the go ahead, especially since having that dream. After all this waiting I would finally find out whether there was something hidden or not.

"Keep me posted on the dig, won't you?" asked Sabberan.

As soon as I put the phone down I rang Karalyn on her Spanish mobile. When she answered she told me that she was in a bar in Cordoba, an old city in Andalucia. She and Rico Santos had left Ugijar and were not likely to be going back for some months.

Oh no. Just when I finally had the green light I was presented with this. They would not be able to dig for months. All that waiting and at the final hurdle this happens.

Time was running out. The convent was starting to fall down and I knew it wouldn't remain standing through another winter. Since the walls were water damaged and it had been hit by lightning, it was deteriorating fast. In fact, it was becoming a bit of a liability and I wanted to sell it on as soon as possible. However it would be such a shame to sell without having tried to dig for the scrolls. When I had tried digging with a group last year we had all got snowed in so we couldn't dig. Then Karalyn and I had tried to dig with our shovels but we didn't have the strength to get anywhere. Then we had asked Rico Santos to dig and Sabberan had stopped that going ahead in case he released another curse. And no sooner had Rico's energy been cleared than I discovered he was no longer living in Ugijar. I needed help. Then inspiration struck. I sent off a whole load of emails to the archae-ology departments of various English Universities, offering them the convent site for a free digging experience.

'Dear X,

In 2004 I decided to set up a yoga center in the Alpujarra mountains in Southern Spain. I bought a semi-derelict convent, intending to use it for yoga. I subsequently discovered this was once home to the Knights Templars.

Due to an unfortunate series of events it is soon to be sold and demolished.

However, before it is demolished I would have loved to explore what lies buried beneath the earth floor, especially as there is so much local legend surrounding this building.

Although the building dates back to at least the 13th or 14th century, it probably has Roman foundations. In the 16th or 17th century it was a Franciscan monastery.

I know nothing about archaeology and would not know how to set about digging. Would you know of anyone who might be interested in this unique opportunity?

Hilary Carter'

Most of them did not reply but those who did were not interested. Not interested in the opportunity to have free rein, digging up the floor of what was once almost certainly a Roman temple and latterly a Knights Templar church? One university (Birmingham) said they might consider it but it would cost me quite a lot to employ them.

I needed to find another way. My next approach was to documentary makers and television producers offering them a chance to make a documentary following the findings of an archaeological dig in a Templar Church.

'Hi

Following a series of coincidences (especially around the number 11 11) I was led to an old convent in southern Spain.

I bought it, and subsequently discovered it had been home to the Knights Templars.

The ancient doors bear the Templar seal.

Five unconnected people have told me of buried scrolls.

I would like to offer involvement in the possible unearthing of these scrolls to a film company.

Would you be interested?'

All the responses were negative. Even the producers of the popular Time Team television show were not interested in digging in a foreign country. I didn't receive many replies. Maybe they thought I was some kind of weirdo making up a story? I even approached the newspapers but not a single one responded.

The words 'head' and 'brick wall' sprung to mind.

Once more I was left waiting and digging was delayed. That convent really did not want to give up its secrets. Whilst I waited for a dig to happen I was also waiting for a buyer to appear. The convent couldn't be on the market forever.

But at least I was beginning to understand the Da Vinci messages. The first message that the convent and Ellingham had given me through the incidents around the number 11 had shown me that winter solstice, December 21st 2012 would be a key day in the history of the Earth. Da Vinci had confirmed this message with the incidences of the number 11 in the Last Supper. What will actually manifest on that day I cannot say, but I believe that the Earth is about to move into a higher vibration. Maybe it will divide in two, into a higher vibration and a lower vibration. Just as, according to the teachings of yoga, we have an etheric counterpart to the physical body, so does the Earth. The 2000-year Age of Pisces is coming to an end and we are about to officially enter the Age of Aquarius. Aquarius is the eleventh sign of the zodiac. Was this the reason that the number 11 was the number that was appearing? Is eleven the cosmic sign for Aquarius appearing? Each zodiacal age lasts about 2000 years. Maybe the book of Revelations has described how the division will take place. Or maybe we won't even notice the shift. We don't have long to wait to find out.

The convent had also led me to another message, revealed by Da Vinci in his paintings of The Last Supper and John the Baptist. This message concerned the role of John the Baptist and his teachings. This message leads us to the path of yoga, an ancient path, tried and tested over many centuries, a safe and effective way of reaching enlightenment.

But the last message, the 33 1 33 grouping in The Last Supper was still niggling me. 33. Where did that come in? What was the 33 message? Was the convent involved in the 33?

'Ugijar 33' as a search on the internet brought up an interesting piece of information. Ugijar was 33 miles from the ancient city of Granada, home to the Moorish masterpiece the Alhambra Palace and capital city of the province of Granada. Ugijar was also 33 miles from Nerja. That must form a triangle. So presumably Ugijar convent forms a grid work in Spain in the same ways as Ellingham does in England. I could pursue the exact layout of the grid another time. Following it now would only be a time consuming distraction. The most important task was to find the core message of the 33.

I was sitting at the kitchen table writing, waiting to give a friend a lift to a yoga workshop. I checked my watch. It was 11.33am. Time to go or we would be late. I was gathering a few bits and pieces of food together for a packed lunch. All the while this 33 was on my mind. What did it mean? Why 33?

I grabbed a muesli bar from the biscuit tin and I was just about to put it in the carrier bag along with the sandwiches and drink when I noticed something. It was called Sirius. Sirius muesli bar. Sirius was also the name of a star. Surely this couldn't be a clue? Was this journey taking me from a tiny country church in Ellingham, Wiltshire, England, to the star called Sirius? Driving to yoga I was stuck behind an elderly lady driver, such a slow car. I noticed her number plate was 133. Looking down at my milometer I saw it read 77333 and the trip meter was at 333. Was I now going to be bombarded by 33 instead of 11 in my everyday life? Was this a sign that my journey had changed from an 11 11 to a 33 journey? Or could it be that the number 33 was the number that was the link to outer space?

As soon as I returned home I continued with my research. Being in the moment helped me to see signs in the most unexpected places, so keeping an open mind (a pre-requisite for this type of journey) I tested out the muesli bar clue and simply typed Sirius 33 into the search engine on the computer.

"The ancient Egyptians began their new year with the rising of Sirius with the sun.

The number 33 has many symbolic implications. The greatest meaning according to Jewish sages is that 33 signifies connection of the material world with the spiritual."

(www.stevequayle.com)

The ancient Egyptians. Builders of the pyramids. I knew that the Great Pyramid in Giza was aligned to Sirius and in ancient Egyptian mythology the star Sirius was represented by the goddess Isis. But in what way did 33 link the material with the spiritual?

In Freemasonry the 33rd degree is the highest degree attainable. The Freemasons must therefore have some knowledge and understanding of the relevance of this number. My research revealed that the "Supreme Symbol" of the 33rd degree of Freemasonry was a double-headed eagle with an illumined triangle balanced on its crown, with a "33" emblazoned within. The double-headed eagle on the door in the convent! Not only the symbol for the Templars but also for the highest Masonic rite. Now I was beginning to wonder what exactly went on behind that beautiful carved door. Maybe the Templars had a connection with the Masonic movement. Were Masons in the convent at some time? Did the Masonic movement grow out of the Templars? The room in the convent with the darkest, densest and most evil energy had two pillars in it, which didn't appear to be structurally necessary. It was only later when I read about the mythology of the Freemasons and Templars, that I discovered one of the core legends was that of Jachin and Boaz – the "Twin Pillars" of Atlantis. All Masonic lodges were constructed with these two pillars at some location in their architecture. They represented the two pillars originally erected at the entrance to King Solomon's Temple in Jerusalem – the Pillars of Jachin and Boaz. Of course the fact that two pillars side by side looked like a number 11 did not escape me.

I also considered how 3 is the first sacred number, "the first perfect number". "Three represents the Pagan Trinity" (Westcott, p41 and p37). It is represented geometrically in the triangle, and spiritually as the Third Eye of Hinduism. Occultists will multiply and add three to other sacred numbers to create new numbers. However, they also group threes in two's and three's, because they believe in the principle of "intensification", that greater power is achieved when a sacred number is grouped. In the case of 3, greater intensification is achieved when it is shown as 33, or 333. 333 + 333 equals 666. Occultists have used 333 as the hidden symbol by which they present the more offensive number 666. When the details of an event are so arranged as to contain certain sacred occult numbers or numeric combinations, this is literally an occult signature on the event. Mathematically, 666 can be created when three pairs of threes are added. Thus, $(3+3) + (3+3) + (3+3) = 666$. Now, eliminate the parentheses and the plus sign, and you have 33 space, 33 space, 33, representing the number 666.

The number 11 is a sacred number. As Wescott explains, "11 is the essence of all that is sinful, harmful, and imperfect." [Westcott, p100]. Thus, while 11 is very important, multiplications are also important, such as 22, 33, 44, 55, 66, 77, 88, and 99.

When eleven is multiplied by the perfect number 3, the number 33 is produced, a number of tremendous occult importance. (www.cuttingedge.org)

'A number of tremendous occult importance.' Whoever built the convent must have known the occult importance of this number. It could not be a coincidence that Ellingham, the convent and the Vatican were involved in an isosceles triangle of 33/33 degrees. An isosceles triangle is one with two sides of equal length. Out of interest I tried drawing a line from the convent directly to the Vatican to see where that line went. The mid-point of the line touched the tip of the island of Minorca. Taking a line from this mid-point at exactly 90 degrees it went slap bang through Rennes Le Chateau, the town at the heart of conspiracy theories made famous by *Holy Blood Holy Grail* and *The Da Vinci Code*. Home to the Cathars at about the same time as my convent was home to the Knights Templars. Now the convent was linked directly to the heart of the mystery of Rennes Le Chateau. The angle of the triangle created between the convent, the Vatican and Rennes was 60 degrees, two 30 degree angles and one 120 degree angle. **(diag 7)**

That was one neat triangle. Two of the sides were exactly the same length so I checked out the distances in kilometres.

According to the AA route finder Ugijar to Rennes Le Chateau is 1195 kilometers or 742.5 miles. Rennes Le Chateau to the Vatican is 1194.7 kilometers or 742.4 miles.

That was design, not accident. One tenth of a mile difference? That was alarmingly accurate and a mind blowing discovery for me, because it brought Rennes Le Chateau right into the magical mystery tour I was on. A flash of inspiration guided me to type these numbers directly into the search engine. And there on my computer screen was a massive clue.

The numbers associated with the tetrahedron, the simplest and most basic of the Pythagorean "perfect solids," are 19.47 or 19.5 and 3 or 33. Exactly the same numbers as the kilometres 1194.7. What were the odds on that? This was no accident! These two numbers were linked to the tetrahedron. And the tetrahedron was linked to the numbers 3 and 33. So the convent was linked to 33 via the tetrahedron. But a tetrahedron was a solid shape. So if I were to take an angle out of Ugijar to create a solid, a tetrahedron, it would take me off the planet. What a curious thought. The only things off the planet are other planets, stars or moons. It momentarily crossed my mind that Sirius might be the 'off the planet' location.

I decided to go back to the NASA website which is where I had found out the time of the 2012 winter solstice. During my search I came across the findings of Richard Hoagland and Michael Bara who had discovered that specific stars were found at particular elevations above the horizon, namely 19.5 and 33.0 degrees but also directly on the horizon and meridian, at the precise moment of a NASA launch or landing.

Why was NASA involved in this? It appeared from their research that NASA had an obsession with the gods and goddesses of ancient Egypt and rocket launches were timed to blast off when certain planets were found in significant positions in the sky. Sirius was particularly significant. Sirius represents the ancient goddess Isis. For example the launch on May 27th 1999 from Cape Canaveral took place when Sirius was at exactly 33 33'. Now I had my link to Sirius. I couldn't help but laugh at the way I was given signs or clues. A muesli bar had led me to this!

NASA obviously knew something it was not revealing publicly. The numbers 33, 333 and 33 33 kept cropping up, strongly linked to the exact time of major events in the space programme. Why are they using this number in such an obvious way? It could be that they had discovered through astrophysics that the numbers had some potency or energy potential. Or it could be for occult reasons, linked to the same powers as the Masons' rituals. What was it they knew? It must have been the same thing that the 33 degree Masons and Da Vinci knew. That was why Da Vinci had grouped the figures in the way he had in *The Last Supper* 3 3 1 3 3. But what was it that they knew? What was the hidden secret message of number 33?

My research reminded me of a system of numbers called binary numbers. I wondered if perhaps there was a clue in the binary numbers. The binary number for 3 is 11. So 3/3 written as a binary number is 11 / 11. The 11 11. In that way the 33 and the 11 11 are linked. There was no doubt about it. Da Vinci's *The Last Supper* was full of 11's and 33's. There was a message in there waiting to be revealed. But what was it? I couldn't get this question out of my mind. It was all I could think about and I knew I wouldn't find peace until it was answered.

CHAPTER TWENTY FIVE

I was on the way to the supermarket when the last piece of the puzzle fell into place. It was only later I recognized what a perfect day it was to have this realization, for the date was June 6th 2006, 06/06/06. Sitting in the car at the traffic lights a sudden moment of illumination came. It just came to me out of nowhere, a sudden knowing.

"Oh my god!" I exclaimed to myself. "That's it!"

I now realized where all this had been leading. I suddenly understood the significance of the 33. I did my shopping in record time, speeding up and down the aisles with my trolley at breakneck speed. At the checkout my change was 3.33 (honest!) I couldn't wait to get home to the Da Vinci art book.

Arriving home I dumped the shopping on the kitchen floor and opened the Da Vinci book at the painting of *The Last Supper*. The answer lay in the picture in front of me. I had the map showing Ellingham, Ugijar and the Vatican perfectly lined up, divided by 33 degrees with the dividing line going straight through the Vatican. Then I had *The Last Supper* with its two groups of three on either side of Jesus, Jesus representing the dividing line. And that V shape near the middle, the gap between Mary Magdalene and Jesus, the angle that had given me the 90 degree clue that had led me to the Vatican representing the 'V'.

I knew it was the Vatican that had pulled the wool over our eyes. They had twisted the story of Jesus to their own ends. I had already figured out that that the church had stolen our Divinity. But that elusive 33 was the final clue.

I knew the 33 was strongly linked to Freemasonry and the 33 degree initiation, and also to Sirius, but who was behind Freemasonry? The Illuminati of course. Da Vinci was telling us that the Vatican was their home.

This was not the conclusion I had wanted to come to. But my intuition told me that the Illuminati were the ones behind all this. I had first read about them 20 years ago in a book trilogy known as the *Illuminatus Trilogy*. I had read these books because the authors Robert Shea and Robert Anton Wilson, had discussed the number 23 which at that time was appearing in my life in such a dramatic way that I had been taken to the edge of my sanity. What better place for the Illuminati to hide than in the very heart of the Catholic church? The church which posed as a teacher of light but was actually preventing millions of people from realizing the truth.

The Illuminati, with 111 as the first three letters of their name.

Then I had another realization. Ellingham had the number 11 in its name.

E(11)ingham. So did Ugijar! Ugijar used to be known as Uxixar. The name Ugijar was a relatively new translation. Once a Roman town, it had within its name the 11 in Roman numerals. U(xi)xar. Ellingham and Uxixar. 11/xi. 11.11.

Who were they, these mysterious group known as the Illuminati? And how were they linked with Freemasonary?

The term Illuminati often refers to an alleged organization that controls world affairs behind the scenes. Illuminati is sometimes used synonymously with New World Order.

And the New World Order is bad news.

Probably the most notorious Freemason lodge is the P2 lodge in Italy. This group has been implicated in everything from bribery to assassinations. P2 is directly connected to the Vatican, the Knights of Malta, and to the US Central Intelligence Agency. It is powerful and dangerous. The P2 lodge has succeeded in infiltrating the Vatican and has scored a coup of tremendous significance – the Pope, John Paul II, has lifted the ban against Freemasonry. Many high-level members of the Vatican are now Freemasons.

Freemasonry is a powerful organization and the Masons are major players in the struggle for world domination. The 33rd degree is split into two. One split contains the core of the Luciferian Illuminati and the other contains those who have no knowledge of it whatsoever. (reference: illuminati-news.com)

It is split into two, just like the groups of figures in *The Last Supper*, the two groups of three split by the sole figure of Jesus. Just like the angle of the triangle coming out of the Vatican, 33 degrees to Ugijar and 33 degrees to Ellingham.

Then there was the 90 degree angle between Jesus and Mary Magdalene. The square and the compass is the sign of the Masonic movement, the square of 90 degrees. Right at the center of *The Last Supper* is this enormous clue of Masonic connections. Hand movements, holding the hand in certain ways, and strange handshakes are all strongly associated with the Masons. And hands are such an overwhelming feature of *The Last Supper* that we are being presented with another Masonic clue. But that's not all. There is the hand being held at the throat of Mary in a somewhat threatening manner. What's going on there? During a Masonic initiation ceremony the right hand thumb is placed to the left of the windpipe and drawn across in a cutting motion.

So this is a blatant Masonic sign from Da Vinci. There can surely be no other reason for such a strange gesture being used in the painting.

Then there is the dagger. I had thought earlier that the dagger had been put there to make the eleventh digit in that area of the painting, with Da Vinci taking every opportunity to drive home the 'eleven' message. I still think thought this was the case but I thought that there was a secondary meaning, namely that the masons were implicated in the story of *The Last Supper*.

Again we need to look at the secret world of Masonic initiations. In some initiations the candidate would be questioned about his eligibility to join with a dagger blade pressed to his throat. Although the dagger was apparently not always used in American lodges, it is still used in United Grand Lodge of England [UGLE] rituals.

Freemasons at the lower degrees of initiation are no doubt going to be appalled that anybody could think that the Masonic movement was evil. Those at the lower levels are often good people who would not harm a soul, those who think that masonry is a positive force in the world. That's because they don't know what goes on at the highest level, the level of the 33rd degree, and 'The 33rd Degree is split into two.' And even at the very highest degree at least half of them don't know what is behind it all.

I recalled one of Psychic Sue's students saying that there had been abortions at the convent and I had thought she was way off the mark. But once I started reading about 33 degree Masons I begin to think she might have stumbled upon the truth. If the Masons were the forerunners of the Templars, which I now believed they were, then abortions might well have taken place in the building, because in black magic foetuses, babies and children were used in certain dark rituals. The Templars were believed to have had knowledge of various ways to procure abortions. I recalled the strange square altar in the back room of the convent and I got the uncomfortable feeling that it wasn't just pigs that had been killed and drained of their blood. The more I read, the more things started to fall into place. At all the Masonic lodges meetings take place when the sun is at its highest, at its meridian. In other words, at midday.

"Freemasons today claim always to meet symbolically at noon on the basis that Freemasonry is a worldwide organisation and therefore 'the sun is always at its meridian with respect to Freemasonry'. Masonic reference to God as 'the most high' is therefore a description of Ra, the sun god in his ultimate position, the zenith of the heavens at noon."

Christopher Knight & Robert Lomas, *The Hiram Key: Pharaohs, Freemasons and the Discovery of the Secret Scrolls of Jesus.*

The very first time I had stepped into the convent with Katarina, the German estate agent, it had been exactly midday because the bells had been ringing their midday serenade as the key was put into the lock. When I became the owner of the convent and opened that ancient door for the first time, again it was exactly noon. Then when I stepped into the local estate agents to put the convent up for sale, once more the bells had been chiming 12. Calle de los Meridas was the address of the convent. This was the road of the Meridian. This was one of the oldest streets in Ugijar. I know that it must have been named thus on purpose.

Realizing what was behind the 33 was such a major breakthrough. I knew it seemed crazy but the 33 was the number that took us off the planet because of its link with NASA and its space program. When I looked at the background of Da Vinci's painting of Virgin of the Rocks it didn't look anything like an earthly landscape. I have had this painting hanging on my wall for several years and I have always looked at it and thought *where on earth is that painting supposed to be set?* Now I knew it was not supposed to be on Earth. It was supposed to be another planet. Maybe it depicted a Sirian landscape? The more I looked at Da Vinci's paintings, the more I saw this repeated theme of the strange rocky, unearthly landscape. It was there in the Annunciation, Little Madonna, The Madonna of the Carnation, Virgin and Child with Saint Anne, the painting of Saint Jerome and even The Mona Lisa.

This was not Earth. Da Vinci was not a prolific painter and there are only a few dozen paintings and drawings of his in existence. Interestingly, one of these drawings is a chart of the distance from the Sun to the Earth and the size of the Moon which is held at the Royal library in Windsor Castle. He was even drawing outer space!

What about the portrait of John the Baptist, his enigmatic expression as he points skywards? There's no unearthly background here because Da Vinci wants us to focus on the message John the

Baptist is giving us with his hands. Like a veil lifted from my eyes, the painting revealed its secret clearly and simply to me. John the Baptist was pointing his finger upwards towards the sky. He was pointing to outer space to tell us that is where the answers lay. We are most definitely not the only intelligent life in the universe. And I think that statement will soon be proved.

It was Carl Sagan who argued for the likely existence of intelligent life elsewhere in the universe. The film *Contact*, released after his death, describes the first encounter between mankind and an alien civilization. This contact was received in the form of a binary code received by radio telescope. This is how most scientists predict we will ultimately make contact with an alien intelligence. With 3/3 translating as 11 11 in binary code, I believe that either individuals are being contacted by aliens through the 11 11 or that our consciousness, once awakened and expanded, begins to encompass intelligence from outer space.

What about John the Baptist's other hand? His other hand pointed to the center of his chest in the gesture that is familiar to all of humanity because it is the gesture we all use to indicate 'I'. Try it for yourself and see. When asked to indicate 'I', nobody points to their nose, their neck or other body part. They all point to this part of their chest, which, in yoga, is the chakra above the main heart chakra known in the Vatican-controlled religion of Catholicism as the Sacred Heart. In the yoga teachings it is this second heart chakra which connects us to our spirit and our true Self.

We actually have three levels of the heart, each one serving a completely different function. The physical heart is the one we all know about, the one that keeps us alive. When our heart stops beating we die. The heart is the one organ in the body that never gets cancer. The second heart belongs to the subtle or etheric body and is known in yoga as the heart chakra. This is the chakra that links you with your Divine Purpose on earth. The third heart is little known and belongs in the realms of esoteric yoga. This is the 'Throne of Power', the gateway to the whole universe. This is how you may understand the nature of your three hearts: The first rules all things physical and emotional; the second, or subtle heart, rules all things spiritual; the third, or Sacred heart, simply rules all things. It is the bridge that connects you with all reality. (For more on this see James Twynham's website www.manataka.org)

So Da Vinci has John the Baptist pointing to himself and to outer space in the same painting. Meaning either 'I come from outer space' or 'I am going to outer space' or 'the answer is in outer space'.

I didn't want it to be this way because it's not an easy concept to digest. It would have been so much easier to end this book at the point where John the Baptist is a yogi and we can all follow the path of yoga to reach enlightenment. That would probably be a leap too far for a lot of people but outer space... that's really stretching belief. Even I was finding it hard. Yet it was all coming together like a huge jigsaw puzzle so I needed to take this journey to its conclusion, palatable or not.

If I took this journey to its extreme limits I would have to take seriously the message that David Icke was communicating. This was a guy that I had down as crazy. Why? Because I read that in the newspapers. Had I read any of his books cover to cover before I had judged him and his ideas? No. He had allowed his mind to consider the unthinkable and to explore ideas and areas that most other people were afraid to. His free-thinking had brought him to virtually the same conclusion that I had been led to by the convent and Ellingham church. That we might think we are free but we are not. Most of us are asleep to the reality of the human situation and it was time to wake up.

I reminded myself about the tetrahedron and the triangle between the Vatican, Rennes Le Chateau and the convent. Was the convent once used to connect to energies or entities off the planet? That's the conclusion I was reaching. I believe that the source of the controller who pulls the strings of world affairs is off the planet.

My first thought was that it is Mars, in view of the fact that Mars is closer to the earth than it has been for 60000 years. Mars, the planet of war. But it could be Sirius.

'As we first reported to you last year, we believe that the world has crossed a Rubicon into a new and extremely dangerous phase. The portent of this new period was defined by the passing of Sirius across the Giza meridian at precisely 12:00 midnight on January 1, 2000, an event which we have shown could not have been "coincidental." At that time, we asserted that this singular event, dictated by a series of deft manipulations of the western Gregorian calendar, had been planned and worked towards for perhaps more than two millennia. The authors of this extraordinary and meticulously planned celestial event were a series of groups which have come to be loosely known as "secret societies" – semi-hidden bands of hand picked and self-appointed "leaders" who frequently attempt to manipulate secular political events.' TheEnterpriseMission.com

As I wrote these words in August 2006 there were two wars dominating the headlines. The first was the ongoing conflict in Iraq, centered on Bhagdad. Bhagdad lies at 33 degrees north. There were also British troops in Basra (30 30'north).

One of the main hot spots for conflict on this planet is the border of Israel and the Lebanon, which was the location of the 33 day war in the summer of 2006. The border lies at 33 33' latitude. (Incidentally this border is 333 km from the Pyramids). Beirut was severely bombed during this war. The latitude of Beirut? 33 north. There were also British troops in Afghanistan; 3300 men were sent out in January 2006, concentrated in the Helmand province. The 33 line of latitude runs through this province.

Coincidence? I don't think so!

"A bleed valve for negative energies". That was how Sabberan had described the convent.

"It's within a vortex of negative energy". That was how psychic Sue had described it.

"A feeding place for forces of darkness" is my own description.

There are grids of light and grids of dark. It has to be so, for in this world of duality light is defined by darkness and vice versa. Ugijar is on a junction of the grids but because of the vast amount of violence/torture/murder/black magic that took place in the convent over the years a vortex of negative (dark) energy had been created. This was so solid and impenetrable that light was unable to flow through the light grid. So, as Sabberan had explained, the light grid as far afield as Egypt and Rome had been affected by the block at Ugijar.

The grids are multi-layered, ranging from the large, structured grid right down through varying degrees of fineness until they are like the finest cobwebs. Imagine being blindfolded and walking into a room thick with cobwebs spun by spiders of all sizes. That is what it was like walking into the convent!

In yoga terms the opposing grids can be referred to as the upper astral plane and the lower astral plane. The upper astral plane is full of light and love and the lower astral is full of hate, evil and darkness. This lower astral plane is home to entities which feed off negative energy. That is what I felt in the convent. That's why I always had such an uncomfortable feeling when I was in there. At some level I could feel the presence of these entities because what better place for them to hang out than at a bleed valve for negative energy? A bit like those fish that feed from the sewage outlets in the sea, huge shoals of them feeding off waste matter where it is released into the ocean. These dark entities take their energy from the lower astral plane and in those places were the energy is thick with darkness, they can feast on evil and therefore continue to exist. No wonder they didn't want me there to remove the darkness and break up their banquet!

Yoga teachings teach us that we need to follow the guidelines of the eight limbs in thought, word and deed, because we are the ones that create the astral planes. The astral planes are a sum total of our thoughts, words and deeds. So it is up to us, as one consciousness, to decide which grid will dominate.

There is a battle between the forces of darkness and the forces of light. It appears to be happening outside of ourselves in the world, but it is really happening inside ourselves. Pain, suffering, fear, distress, ignorance, hatred, anger, depression, grief and violence feed the lower astral plane. What better way to create a plethora of these emotions than war. War is a fertile feeding ground for the dark entities. So the Illuminati manipulate the world and create wars. Holy wars and inquisitions. They create religions with their narrow dogma which cause potentially good people to kill and maim each other in the name of God. All that fear and emotional distress and trauma is exactly what the lower astral planes, and the entities that reside there, want. They feed from the negative emotions and grow stronger.

What's more, there are certain places on earth that are more powerful than others. These are the places where the grids cross and interact. Any events happening at these key sites have a much more marked effect on the state of the grids than events not at a junction. Places such as the convent are built on the junctions of the grid. In fact I would go as far as to say that all ancient churches and temples are built on psychically sensitive points. When praise, goodness, holiness and ceremonies of light are being performed at these places then the grid of light is strengthened. But massacres and black magic rituals at these same locations feed the darkness. Events such as the Holy Inquisition were a huge coup for the dark energies because of all the negative vibrations that were set up on so many important junctions in a relatively short space of time. After all, the Inquisition homed in on abbeys, convents and monasteries all of which were built on junctions. The convent in Ugijar was a perfect example. I had recalled my own fear as I was tortured in the convent during the Inquisition. I was only one of many thousands of people pouring fear, pain and distress into the grid. The Inquisition had been followed by the Muslim uprising in Granada in the seventeenth century when a massacre had taken place in Ugijar. The accumulative power of these negative vibrations was so great that, as Sabberan said, places as far afield as Egypt, Israel and France had been directly affected. So whoever has possession and control of the most important junctions on the grid has more influence on the grid as a whole. I suspect the Vatican must be built on a seriously major junction.

It is an indisputable fact that Israel, Britain and the US in particular are involved in wars along the 33degree of latitude.

It seems as if for some reason the Illuminati want or need to create a negative emotional field along this line of latitude. My guess would be that this is the point of connection between earth and other planets, probably Sirius or Mars. It could possibly be an insertion point for aliens. I know it's a challenging thought to consider but we need to think out of the box if we are to break through and wake up!

11 11 is the sign of light that leads us along the higher path. It is the finger pointing the way, showing us where we are to go if we are to fulfil our mission on earth. It can lead us to dark places (like the convent!) and in this way can appear to be dark but it isn't. From my experiences 33 33 appears to be the number of the Illuminati, hence its appearance in war zones, Freemasonary, and the NASA launches to Mars, the planet of war.

11 11 is a binary number which I believe is the number of a higher consciousness.

33 33 is NOT a binary number and as such it is the untransformed 11 11.

There is a huge clue there. If the earth is to divide into different vibrations in 2012, those who choose to follow the untransformed 33 will be choosing that darker vibration whilst those who follow the 11 11 may be able to enter a doorway into other dimensions. 11 11 could be called the pin code that opens the lock on the doorway to other realities.

As I said earlier, I don't know what will manifest on Winter Solstice 2012. It could be that a sealing spell/time lock on the earth itself will be released, allowing a cosmic doorway to open. Whether the open door will be immediately apparent on that day or not I cannot say. However, my belief is that a huge expansion of consciousness will take place and our experience of reality will expand beyond anything we can imagine. If life is multi dimensional maybe we will have different experiences of reality.

The numbers and angles between the convent, the Vatican, Ellingham and Rennes Le Chateau were the same as the numbers and angles hidden in Da Vinci's The Last Supper. Why would Da Vinci have put the clues there? That painting is hundreds of years old and nobody has ever spotted the relevance of these numbers and angles. Until now.

In my own frame of reference, now is the end of the Age of Pisces and the beginning of the Age of Aquarius, the approach of 2012. It is as if the hidden code could not be broken until the time was right, and the right time is now.

I believe DaVinci discovered the truths that we are now starting to wake up to as we approach 2012. He knew about 2012 and the 11 11 code. He knew that John the Baptist was the Keeper of the Truth and that Jesus was not the true teacher. John the Baptist was. He knew that humanity had been led away from the truth of their own Divinity by the Illuminati-created religion of Christianity.

John the Baptist came to earth as a teacher, not as a prophet. The legacy and teachings of John the Baptist are currently being kept alive by the Mandean people who live on the border of Iran and Iraq. Of all the places on earth they could have ended up, they are to be found living at 33 degrees of latitude. As we approach the critical date of 2012, these peace loving people and their knowledge are in danger of being lost due to living in a war zone.

The Vatican, being under the control of the dark forces, had created a mind-control religion, Catholicism, to keep people blinkered to the truth. As Freemasonary is divided even at the 33rd degree I believe that when DaVinci discovered the alarming truth, possibly during his time in Rome, then he had a dilemma.

If he had announced his findings during his lifetime then very few people would have got to know about his discovery. He might even have been killed and the knowledge buried along with him. But if he could somehow keep his revelations secret until the approach of 2012 then his knowledge would stand a much better chance of being revealed to the masses, thereby giving humanity the opportunity to wake up en masse. By the end of the twentieth century the majority of humanity would be more able to hear the awful truth, that we are pawns in the game of life and will continue to be so unless we stop buying into the game. Thanks to the internet, the media and the literacy of so many people in this century, DaVinci's hitherto hidden discoveries could not easily be hidden from the world if revealed near to 2012.

During my research for this book I read that Da Vinci would spend many hours standing in front of his painting of *The Last Supper*. He was probably asking himself whether the clues were clear enough to be seen when the time was right, without being too obvious. If they were too obvious they would have been spotted too early. I am certain that DaVinci had the occult knowledge that I once had and so he would probably have put a sealing spell on the painting with a 'sell by' date on it, knowing that once the figure of Mary Magdalene was recognized, then the true code of The Last Supper and his other paintings would be free to be revealed. From that would come the truth that John the Baptist was the true teacher, not Jesus. We have been 'spun a yarn' for two thousand years.

One of the psychics I came across on my journey had said, "You will find what you are looking for." At the time I had assumed that she meant that I would find scrolls hidden under the floor of the convent. Or I would find the valuable artefacts that I had swept up in a cloth and hurriedly buried before I was captured and killed in another life in the convent. Nothing like that has yet been found, but I realize I have found something else. I have found a much deeper understanding of what is actually happening on this planet.

CHAPTER TWENTY SIX

At last I had a buyer for the convent. I was so relieved, because it had become a huge liability as more and more of this ancient building was crumbling to the ground. The torrential rain had damaged the earth walls to such an extent that they were past repair. My concern was that the façade had become so weakened it might collapse into the road. The buyer was a Spanish property developer who intended demolishing the convent and building apartments on the site. He wanted to proceed quickly with the sale so, early in October I flew out to Almeria to sign the deeds and finally draw this whole convent scenario to a close. The developer had paid a ten per cent deposit to Katarina, the agent I had bought it through originally, so I knew he was a serious buyer. When I arrived in Spain I called in at Katarina's office.

"You have the escitura, the deeds, yes?" she asked.

My heart sank.

"No. I didn't realize I would need them," I replied.

"Oh dear. It would be much better if we had them. But it is not a huge problem. It means that we will have to sign the deeds in Ugijar. My client was wanting to sign in Almeria city but now he must come to Ugijar. Don't worry Hilary. I will arrange that as soon as possible."

Leaving it in Katarina's capable hands I headed off to the beach where I lay on the sand by the edge of the sea. Even though it was October, the weather was beautiful. I loved this climate. The next day I called in to see Katarina again. I could see from her face it was bad news.

"You will not believe this," she said, "but the only day the signing can take place in Ugijar is on Wednesday. And the only day that my client cannot come and sign is Wednesday. He is in Murcia on that day and cannot cancel his appointment."

"So I will have to come back again."

I was not annoyed or upset. I had learned that the best attitude in a situation like this was acceptance. I couldn't change the situation so I just accepted it.

"Unless you can stay for longer and we can do it next Wednesday?" she asked hopefully.

"No. I can't. I'll have to go back to England and return in a few weeks."

"But my client wants to proceed with the building work before the bad winter weather sets in. He needs to make the building safe before the rains. He does not want a huge delay so you will have to come back really soon," she warned me.

"I realize that. I'll come back in the beginning of November, the middle of the month at the latest." That was in three weeks time.

Lying by the sea I silently asked why this should have happened. Why should there be a delay at this late stage? Was this a lesson in patience or a test of acceptance? Why? My question reverberated out into the universe and the answer came back within seconds.

It's to give you one last chance to unearth the scrolls.

Of course! It was so obvious. I knew I had been given a three-week window which would be my very last opportunity to arrange a dig. I didn't know how I was going to do it but I was sure I would be shown a way....

The next day I took the local bus up the mountain to Ugijar. It was an old, noisy bus and the front windscreen was seriously cracked. It looked like maybe it had been hit by a falling rock. The driver looked to either side of the cracks as he drove, craning his neck as he peered first to one side and then to the other. At he drove he was carrying on a conversation with the only other two passengers, one of whom was leaning on the back of his seat and the other who stood next to him as he maneuvered the long, old vehicle round the sharp bends in the mountain roads. I had arranged to meet my friend Claire in Ugijar to catch up on news. She was waiting by the church as the bus pulled into town. It was pretty empty as the weather up here was very different to the warmth of the coast. Up here at this high altitude it was misty and there was a cold drizzle. I wished I had worn a coat. As I stepped from the bus the church bells began to chime. The moment my foot touched the tarmac of the main road in Ugijar, the clock struck its first bell. As I walked across the square to greet Claire, the sound of the bells reverberated in my ears. We hugged and the bells stopped.

"11."

"I know. The bus is a bit late," said Claire.

"No. 11. The bells were chiming 11!" I exclaimed. What a magical greeting. The bells tolled for me and I knew it.

We headed for the bar which sold the best tapas and we sat on the high stools eating warm toasted goats cheese with crushed tomatoes mixed with local olive oil and pungent garlic in freshly baked bread.

"How did the signing go? Have you sold it now?" asked Claire.

"No. You're not going to believe this but I forgot to bring the escitura so we can't sign. I'm going to have to come all the way back to Spain again in a couple of weeks!"

"Oh no, that's awful."

"No it's not. I know why it's happened. It's to give me a final chance to find those scrolls. I've got three weeks to find them. All I've got to do is find somebody who can dig for me."

"How about Rico Santos? I thought he was going to dig."

"He can't, he's in Cordoba with Karalyn."

"No he's not. They're just down the road in Cherin. They came over for the fiesta and haven't gone back yet."

What luck. Well, no, it wasn't luck but perfection.

"That's fantastic. The only thing is, although I think I know where the scrolls are, I have no idea how deep they are. They could be so deep that Rico Santos will never find them. What I need to do is find somebody who can dowse and tell me how deep they are. Do you dowse?" I asked.

"No, not really. What about you? Surely you could dowse."

"I can't. It's something I've tried but I just can't get the hang of it."

We sat in silent thought. It could take months to dig up that floor. We really needed a clear idea of where they were and how deep they were before we started.

"That's an interesting necklace."

Claire's voice broke my train of thought. She was talking to the woman standing next to her at the bar.

"Yes," replied the woman, "It represents the Goddess energy."

Claire looked me in the eye and I looked back, a conversation without words. We knew it all in that moment.

"Do you dowse?" I asked the stranger.

"Yes I do. I heal, clear spaces and dowse for lost objects. That is the work I do all over the world. I am only here in Ugijar for a couple of hours, I'm just passing through."

She handed me her business card. '*Where miracles begin*' it said in German. The background was a picture of Stonehenge, the famous stone circle in Wiltshire, England. As a child I had often played in the center of this ancient monument, before the days of fences and security guards. I remembered lying on the large flat stone which had fallen onto its side and I had played chase around the standing stones with my brothers and sisters on long, sunny, summer days.

These coincidences were not lost on me. Like the dowser, I too was only in town for a few hours – the last bus out of town was at 5pm. And so it was that half an hour later I found myself in the convent with Claire, Hotahara the dowser, her partner and their large dog.

"So we need to get clear before we start." Hotahara was German and talked in a clear, loud, firm voice. "My fee for this will be 100 euros." Claire and I looked at each other. I didn't like what was happening.

"I wasn't expecting you to want payment."

"Why not? This is the way I earn my living. This is a very good price. Normally I charge up to three and a half thousand."

"Yes but I'm not out to make a personal profit from this. I simply want to find the scrolls so that the information they contain can be used to help humanity."

"Tell me Hilary. How do you earn a living?"

"I teach yoga".

"And do you charge for this?"

"Yes."

"Well I charge for my dowsing. It is 100 euros. You can take it or leave it. I don't mind."

I felt intensely uncomfortable and acutely aware that this was a test. But what was it a test of? Was it a test to see if I could allow money to flow or was it a test to see if I was going to follow my intuition or my mind? I didn't know. What I did know was that I felt uncomfortable with this. Yet what an opportunity. If I turned this down surely I would always regret it? Would I always think that I got to the last days of this adventure with the convent only to fail at the last hurdle because I wouldn't part with a mere 100 euros?

Claire could not help me. This was my journey, my story, my money, my feelings and my test. I decided to go with my gut feeling. I had ignored my intuition before and lived to regret it. I simply could not ignore this uncomfortable feeling in my tummy. It took courage but I did it all the same.

"It doesn't feel right." I stated. "It just doesn't feel right."

Hotahara was not fazed.

"That's okay. That's your choice. It really doesn't matter to me. But Hilary I will say this to you. You are not clear. If you had really wanted to find those scrolls you would not have hesitated. You would have given me 10,000 euros if you were clear because you would not have cared about anything except finding the scrolls."

Who knows if she was right or not? Anyway, I had made my

decision based on my intuition and I stood by it. We were standing just inside the entrance hall of the convent beside the open door. Then Hotahara noticed Claire's bracelet.

"Let me see your bracelet," Hotahara said to Claire, lifting Claire's arm and examining her silver and copper bracelet. It was a copper bracelet inscribed in silver with a yoga mantra, Om Namah Shivaya, written in an Indian script. This mantra was the mantra of Babaji, the immortal yogi written about in *Autobiography of a Yogi* by Paramhansa Yogananda. This is the book that I had read and re-read when I had first arrived in these mountains. I had a picture of Babaji on my bedside table and when I had visited Claire's retreat center higher up the mountain I had seen that she had the same photo of him as me.

Hotahara took hold of Claire's hand and examined it briefly then she silently pulled up the sleeve of her own jumper to reveal the bracelet on her own arm. It was an exact replica of Claire's. Identical in every detail.

"Babaji!" we all said in unison, adopting the same whispered tone of awe.

"I've changed my mind. I want you to dowse."

There was no hesitation in my voice. Now I was clear. I knew that this was a sign. My test had been to see if I would follow my intuition. Now I was being given a strong and clear sign to show me my next move. We all laughed, even the dog seemed to be laughing. I had known intelligent dogs before but this one had an almost human presence about him.

"He's an ashram dog," explained Hotahara. "From the Babaji ashram."

Closing the main door behind us we moved to the entrance hall and pulled up some old chairs and a discarded box and stool to sit on. We formed a circle, held hands and we began to chant. Ohm.... we chanted, one after the other, until the entire convent was vibrating to the sound of this sacred mantra. The sound filled the building, then the street, then the valley, then the mountains. As the vibration increased, my heart began pounding furiously, just like the time when I had first entered the convent with Karalyn. This was curious. Why should my heart be pounding like this. We seemed to know when to stop the chant, as if we were one consciousness.

"Okay. You two can stay here and we will go and dowse."

Hotahara and her partner headed off to the back of the convent followed by the dog. I turned to Claire.

"This is not about finding the scrolls Claire. This is about healing me."

Why else would my heart be beating so hard that it felt as if it would burst? This was something that involved my heart. Claire and I sat in silence whilst the others went exploring, Hotahara with her dowsing crystal. After about ten minutes we were called.

"Hilary, Claire, come!"

They were in the second room from the front, not the room where I had believed the scrolls to be. Hotahara pointed to the floor.

"They are here," she said with an air of authority. "Right there at a depth of between one and a half and two meters." She pointed down to the earth floor about a meter away from the high window.

"Come and stand here, Hilary. Stand there directly above the scrolls."

I obediently stood where I was told. Somehow I had known this was coming. Hotahara's partner stood behind me and Claire and Hotahara stood either side of me. I was glad they were there because for some reason my legs had turned to jelly and they were shaking like mad. "Now close your eyes and tell me what you feel."

I closed my eyes and for a minute I felt nothing. We were standing in silence. Then from out of nowhere I had the feeling that I had been struck viscously from behind by a heavy object which I recognized as a metal candle holder, and I realized I had once more gone back in time, back to the life when I was a Templar. They must have caught me in the tunnel after I had hidden the scrolls.

"What is happening, Hilary?" asked Hotahara.

"They must not find the scrolls. They must not get them."

"Who mustn't get them?"

"The church. They must not fall into the hands of the church."

My legs were shaking like crazy and they just wouldn't stop. My heart was still pounding too.

"What will happen if the church gets them?"

"The church will destroy them to hide the truth."

"Why? What is written in these scrolls?"

"The truth."

"What is the truth, Hilary?"

"The truth is that religion is not the truth. We are Divine. We don't need a church to know the truth. The church doesn't want us to know our own Divinity. We are love. That's our true nature but nobody wants to know that. The time is not right. I have to keep the scrolls safe until the time is right."

"Who will you give them to if you find these scrolls?"

"To humanity."

"And what difference will it make if the church gets hold of these? Because the church cannot hide the truth. You know the truth is that you are love. You carry the truth with you wherever you go. You are the love. Why spend time searching for scrolls, for information, for proof, when you already have the answer? Why waste time? Precious time you are wasting looking while you could spend the time just being, being love. "

My eyes filled with tears which fell heavily onto the floor, seeping into the earth above the scrolls. I felt such compassion for the person I had been in that life, when I had undertaken my mission with such sincerity, giving up my life in order to protect those scrolls and the information they contained. Little did I realize when I had hidden them that it would take me almost a thousand years to come back for them.

"Because I want everyone to know the truth."

"It's time to walk away, Hilary. They didn't want to hear about love in that life. You tried to teach them but they didn't want to know. Instead they killed you. Are you ready to leave the scrolls behind and be love?"

I nodded my head. "Yes," I whispered, the tears still falling. The three of them held me lovingly, giving me strength and support. They were demonstrating universal love in action.

I was ready to leave it all behind. It was as if I was drawing a line under my life (or lives…) and as I walked out of the convent I felt so much lighter as if I had finally been released from that cobwebby energy that had sucked me in to that place. I walked away without a backward glance and I knew I would never set foot in the convent again, not in this life nor in any other life.

As I walked away I could see that new people had moved into the building opposite and they were busy renovating Karalyn's place. Karalyn had had to move out because of the occult activity in there. The new owners were English but the builders were Spanish. They were converting the downstairs into a new apartment. I just hoped they were not too psychic.

I was just in time to catch the five o'clock bus and as we drove back down the mountain I could see a rainbow of light in the sky. It was not curved and, unlike a rainbow, it was on the same side of the sky as the sun. Normally a rainbow was directly opposite the sun. It remained there until the bus reached sea level at the town of El Ejido.

Back in my hotel room I had a shock when I looked in the mirror, for a raised triangular mark had appeared in the center of my forehead in the exact location of the ajna chakra, also known as the third eye. It was a bit like a spot, but triangular. It remained there for about 24 hours and then disappeared.

Once I was safely back in England, a few days later I phoned Karalyn, who was in Picena, about 20 minutes from Ugijar. She agreed to ask Rico Santos to dig.

"Did you hear about my old place?" she asked.

"Hear what? I saw the new people who were starting to make a new apartment downstairs."

"Yesterday I was in Ugijar and I called in to say hello, but the owners weren't around. Only the builders were there and they were really on edge. Apparently when they were putting in the new drains for the new apartment they dug down and came across the entrance to a tunnel. It was a proper entrance with curved brickwork in the traditional Arabic style so it must have been ancient."

"You're joking!"

"No I'm not. I told you that Rico Santos had said there was a tunnel between the convent and my place."

"Did you see it for yourself then?"

"No, because as soon as they had uncovered it strange things started to happen. Tools were moved, stuff went missing – just disappeared off the face of the earth. And then they heard noises. It frightened the builders so much that they put the drains in quickly and covered it up again. Poor guys. They were really scared."

I was disappointed that she had not managed to get a photo to prove the existence of the tunnel. But I need not have worried because although I didn't realize it at the time, proof of the tunnel was on its way.

I was back in Spain a few weeks later on the 11th November: 11/11. This time the signing was going ahead. At the last minute the buyer had dropped his offer by more than ten thousand euros, but I was past caring. I was just so desperate to get rid of the place. The signing took place in the city of Almeria. There was me, Katarina, the buyer, the buyer's father and Pedro. It was Pedro who had arranged for Katarina to sell the convent and it was he who had turned the key in the lock as the bells had chimed midday. We sat in the lawyer's office reading through the pile of paperwork. My buyer was a property developer and there was a reference to his company in the papers. I noticed that his company had been inaugurated on 22 02 2002. I pointed this out to him.

"Lots of two's!"

"Oh yes," he replied. I don't think he had noticed that before. That's the thing. If you were not tuned into numbers it was easy to miss huge, obvious signs like that.

The papers were signed. I underlined my signature with a flourish and then nudged the purchaser. "Look at the clock." I whispered. It was 12.22pm.

Then he handed me a cheque. Once all the fees and taxes had been paid I had been left with a neat sum of money. 133000 euros. I had bought the convent for 111000, making a net profit of 22,000 euros!

We left the building and stepped outside into the beautiful November sunshine. Our eyes were drawn to the large flashing light right in front of us. A huge number 22 was flashing madly. This was a massive neon display that showed the temperature. It was just after midday, sunny, and the temperature was obviously 22 degrees! I pointed this out to the buyer. I could see he was frightened. I chose this moment to tell him about the scrolls and where I thought they were hidden.

"If I find them, they are yours," he told me.

It was too late for Rico Santos to start digging. He had missed his chance and anyway, he had moved on to other things.

The five of us sat in a pavement café drinking coffee and now that I had safely offloaded the convent I felt confident enough to tell a bit of what had happened over the preceding two years. Pedro was particularly intrigued. He took a serviette and began to draw a map.

"The tunnel system is quite straight forward," he stated. "There is an entrance inside the hermitage at the entrance of the town. The tunnel goes all the way to the church where there is another entrance. It goes along here," he said, drawing a line right across the old part of Ugijar, "and comes out in the town hall."

"The town hall?"

"Yes. It wasn't always the town hall. It used to be the Guarderia Civil. The Civil Guard offices. Then it goes under here and comes out in the convent, just behind the back stairs."

That was just below the room that I had never entered. So there was an entrance to the tunnel in the convent. Pedro knew this because he had been a senior member of the Civil Guard in the days of Franco. My immediate thought was that they were probably all Freemasons and had used the tunnels in their ceremonies. Had they been involved in black magic? My research on the Masonic movement had revealed that their ceremonies were performed at the meridian.

"*Q. Where were you made a Mason?*

A. In the body of a Lodge, just, perfect and regular.

Q. And when?

A. When the sun was at its meridian.

Q. As in this country Freemasons' Lodges are usually held and candidates initiated at night, how do you reconcile that which at first sight appears a paradox?

A. The sun being a fixed body and the earth continually revolving about the same on its own axis and Freemasonry being a universal science, diffused throughout the hole of the inhabited globe, it necessarily follows that the sun must always be at its meridian with respect to Freemasonry." – description of Masonic ritual.

Calle de Los Meridas was the address of the convent. The word meridas comes from the same source as meridian meaning the midday. I recalled the moment the key was first put into the convent door in my presence, when the bells had tolled midday. Then the first time I entered the convent alone, once again it was exactly midday. But the numbers surrounding the sale of the convent are all to do with the number 2, in particular 22. Was this the next phase of the journey? Was this the even masculine number manifesting now that the convent was owned by a man, because 11 is an odd and therefore feminine number (all even numbers are masculine or yang and all even numbers are feminine or yin) and the 11 was the number that was manifesting for me.

"If I find the scrolls they are yours," repeated the new owner of the convent. "I will make sure you get them."

"Thank you," I said, looking into his dark brown Spanish eyes and wondering what lives he had lived in the convent. Was he one of the nuns that had been massacred? Or had he been an Arab? Or maybe part of the inquisition? He was certain to have had some connection with the convent before. At least now the site was clear of the darkness and I knew that no harm would befall him. I kissed him on each cheek and he walked away, clutching the ancient key in his hand.

I left Spain the following day with total detachment. Anything could happen. The scrolls might never be found. They might be found but not given to me. They might be found but be in such bad condition by now that they were unreadable. Or they might be safely in my hands within a few weeks. It really didn't matter to me what happened for I knew that if I was meant to have the scrolls I would have them. There was nothing I needed to do other than trust that everything was unfolding perfectly.

So I carry on with my life, following signs and being in the moment. I am still pursuing my dream of a yoga center. I have found a property in France. It's a small property and was once part of an ancient convent.

But that's another story.

DIAGRAMS

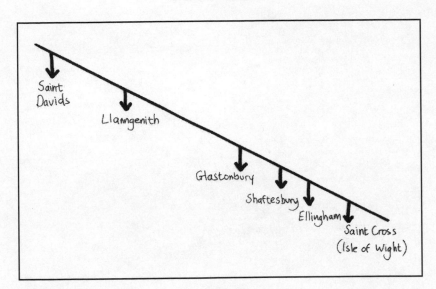

Diagram 1

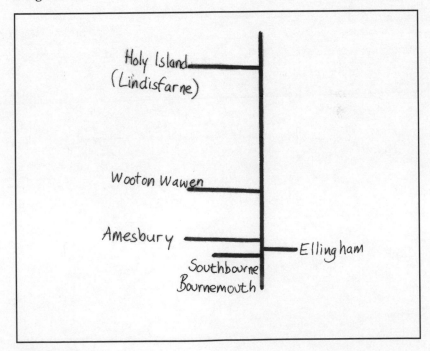

Diagram 2

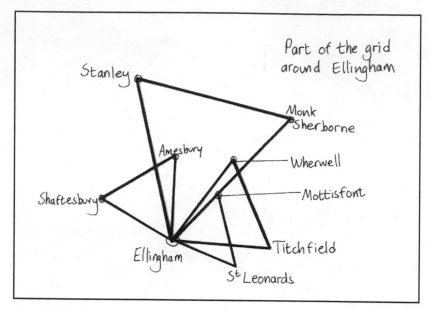

Diagram 3

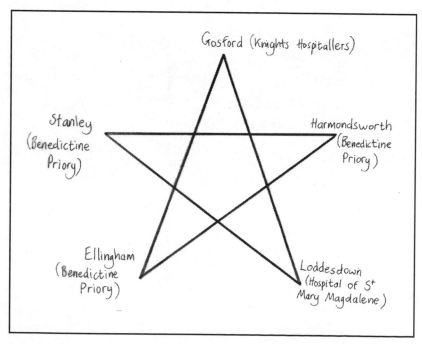

Diagram 4

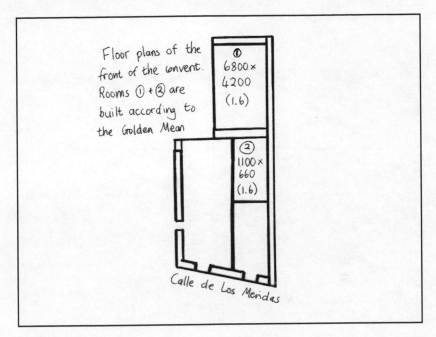

Floor plans of the front of the convent. Rooms ① + ② are built according to the Golden Mean

① 6800 × 4200 (1.6)

② 1100 × 660 (1.6)

Calle de Los Mendas

Diagram 5

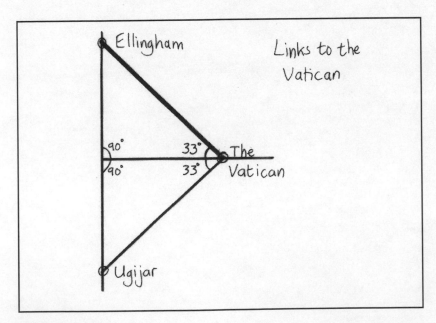

Ellingham

Links to the Vatican

90°
90°
33°
33°
The Vatican

Ugijar

Diagram 6

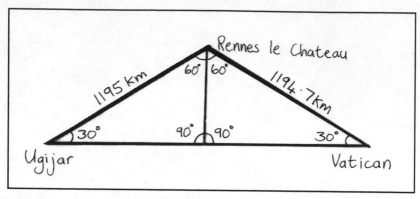

Diagram 7

BOOKS

O is a symbol of the world, of oneness and unity. In different cultures it also means the "eye," symbolizing knowledge and insight. We aim to publish books that are accessible, constructive and that challenge accepted opinion, both that of academia and the "moral majority."

Our books are available in all good English language bookstores worldwide. If you don't see the book on the shelves ask the bookstore to order it for you, quoting the ISBN number and title. Alternatively you can order online (all major online retail sites carry our titles) or contact the distributor in the relevant country, listed on the copyright page.

See our website www.o-books.net for a full list of over 500 titles, growing by 100 a year.

And tune in to myspiritradio.com for our book review radio show, hosted by June-Elleni Laine, where you can listen to the authors discussing their books.

mySpiritRadio